NUCLEAR FREEZE
IN A COLD WAR

A VOLUME IN THE SERIES

Culture and Politics in the Cold War and Beyond

Edited by

EDWIN A. MARTINI

and

SCOTT LADERMAN

Nuclear Freeze in a Cold War

The Reagan Administration,
Cultural Activism, and the
End of the Arms Race

William M. Knoblauch

University of Massachusetts Press
Amherst and Boston

Copyright © 2017 by University of Massachusetts Press
All rights reserved
Printed in the United States of America

ISBN 978-1-62534-275-1 (paper); 274-4 (hardcover)

Designed by Jack Harrison
Set in Adobe Minion Pro with Impact display
Printed and bound by The Maple-Vail Book Manufacturing Group

Cover design by Jack Harrison
Cover art: *Nuclear War* by Razvan Ionut Dragomirescu
montaged with image of vintage TV set. Photos from Shutterstock.

Library of Congress Cataloging-in-Publication Data
A catalog record for this book is available from the Library of Congress.

British Library Cataloguing-in-Publication Data
A catalog record for this book is available from the British Library.

*This book is dedicated with love
to Anna Seidel-Quast.*

Contents

Preface

This is a book about the early 1980s, specifically the politics and culture of the arms race. In 1980, presidential hopeful Ronald Reagan campaigned on promises to stand strong against the Soviet Union. After the American people elected him president, he oversaw the largest nuclear buildup in American history, while his top-ranking officials began bragging about "winning" and "surviving" a nuclear war. In response, the antinuclear movement exploded. Numerous groups, including the Union of Concerned Scientists (UCS), the Physicians for Social Responsibility (PSR), and the Committee for a Sane Nuclear Policy (SANE) all grew in numbers; but none could match, in numbers or popularity, the nuclear freeze campaign. Started by Randall Forsberg, from 1981 to 1984 the nuclear freeze campaign worked to put disarmament referenda on state ballots. With its simple call to halt the arms race, "the freeze" rapidly grew popular. In June 1982 an estimated one million Americans flooded the streets of New York City in the largest peace demonstration in US history.

Instead of grassroots protestors, however, in this book I examine the efforts of a select group of activists, those who used American mass media to criticize Reagan's arms buildup. They include Jonathan Schell, author of *The Fate of the Earth,* and Roger Molander, author of *Nuclear War: What's in It for You?,* whose best-selling books helped to promote and organize record-setting antinuclear protests; the film director Nicholas Meyer, whose antinuclear made-for-TV movie *The Day After* drew in an estimated one hundred million viewers, the largest television audience of 1983; and the celebrity scientist Carl Sagan, who spread warnings of a new threat, a "nuclear winter," which he believed rendered the arms race both illogical and futile. Criticizing the administration in *New York Times* best sellers, on network television, and with multimedia propaganda campaigns, these activists threatened Reagan's arms buildup. Through a combination of archival research, analysis of recently declassified White House documents, and author interviews, I argue that, in time, the efforts of these antinuclear cultural activists influenced the White House to reconsider its rhetoric and publicize a more conciliatory tone in its Cold War diplomacy. In 1982, alarmed at antinuclear media but still determined to continue its arms buildup, the Reagan administration crafted publicity campaigns to co-opt the freeze movement's messages of peace. Their goal was to rebrand President Reagan as a peacekeeper, but in the process the administration also began to shift its thinking; by 1984 the once-empty rhetoric of peace became the genuine goal of an increasingly pragmatic administration.

This is a project many years in the making. It began in 2004 when a flash flood decimated the campus of the University of Hawaii at Manoa, including our graduate offices and the humanities library. Inspired by my newly apocalyptic surroundings—and relegated to online archival resources—I stumbled across discussions of a "nuclear winter." Fascinated by Carl Sagan's efforts to convince the world to disarm, I pursued a full-length project on nuclear winter—that is, until Lawrence Badash's exhaustive *A Nuclear Winter's Tale* preempted my efforts. I was still fascinated by the politics and culture of the atomic 1980s, though, and sharpened my focus one afternoon, thanks to the advice of Lary and Elaine Tyler May, who (over some very strong coffee) encouraged me to follow my interests in atomic popular culture and uncover its connections to politics.

In many ways, this was a natural topic to pursue, as my interest in the atomic 1980s runs deep. Born at the outset of the decade, I remember many of the major events of the Reagan administration, even if I had little understanding of their importance. As a child, I played the video game *Missile Command* on my Atari 2600, watched MTV music videos about how "Everybody Wants to Rule the World," and consumed many late night action movies—too many to name—in which the Russians were always the bad guys and the Americans always won. I recall watching alongside shocked classmates as the *Challenger* exploded on television and later viewing news reports about "Contras" and the US government's wrangling with Iran. Through it all, there was Ronald Reagan—an omnipresent figure, grandfatherly in appearance and measured in tone, always reassuring me that we were the good guys and that America was still the greatest country on earth.

Reagan's unwavering optimism seemed almost sickeningly earnest in my undergrad years as the 1990s came to a close, but such memories are hard to shake. Entering graduate school in the early 2000s, I noticed a growing, almost cultlike veneration for Reagan. He remains an inescapable political figure from our past—the "Teflon President" who could weather accusations of nefarious negotiations with terrorists and without serious consequence ignore congressional directives. I should disclose up front that my own perception of America's fortieth president remains mixed. For me, Reagan was not the flawless executive so often misremembered by contemporary conservatives, nor was he the "amiable dunce" that Democrats loved to deride. Any investigation into the Reagan archives reveals an active and engaging executive, albeit one who—perhaps from natural inclination, or perhaps in the hopes of avoiding the pitfalls of his predecessor, the micromanager Jimmy Carter—preferred to delegate responsibilities to others.

Despite this well-documented leadership style, too often commentators overemphasize Reagan's personal role in ending the Cold War arms race. This book, then, is one attempt to redirect scholarship away from an often-inscrutable president and toward the lesser-known figures who worked to create, publicize, and in time refocus Reagan's vision. Often, these administration officials struggled to contain the popularity of the antinuclear movement, and recently declassified White House documents provide new perspectives on the nuclear freeze movement's potential—as well as cultural activism's role in enacting political change. Previous examinations of the early 1980s have largely assessed antinuclear pop culture (in films, on television, and in print media) as reflections of atomic anxiety, not effective political propaganda; instead, they point to failed congressional efforts to pass meaningful freeze resolutions or applaud the well-meaning efforts of grassroots activists as the historical actors who most pressured the White House to disarm.

The archives, however, tell a much different story—that when it comes to the early 1980s antinuclear movement, popular culture mattered. This was an administration led by a former actor in a White House that reconfigured its Office of Media Relations to deal with new challenges in an era of technological globalization. Time and again, memoranda and correspondence uncovered numerous nervous officials, figures less concerned with sit-ins or protestors and more alarmed at the growing influence of paperbacks, movies, and media ads. Thus, my aim with this book is to reassert pop culture's place in 1980s antinuclear activism and the role it played in the end of the arms race.

A project this long in the making requires many thanks. First, to Paul Schue, Richard Rapson, Michael Amundson, Leilah Danielson, Kevin Mattson, Katherine Jellison, Benita Blessing, Joseph Slade, S. Todd Pfeffer, Patrick McCray, Allan Winkler, Kyle Harvey, Paul Rubinson, Christian P. Peterson, Erica Hannickel, and Elaine Tyler May, all of whom offered suggestions, demanded clarifications, or refocused my thinking at crucial junctures. Chester Pach deserves special thanks; his patience, guidance, and eye for editing remain unparalleled. Tom Engelhardt, Richard Turco, Brian Toon, Ann Druyan, Bob Derkach, Ron Wood, and Pamela Ronsaville all offered valuable time for interviews; Martin Klimke, Jeremi Suri, and Lawrence Wittner each provided detailed commentary for chapters-in-progress which sent my research and writing in exciting new directions. Sadly, since this book began we've lost some fine scholars, including Timothy Moy, Jonathan Schell, and Paul Boyer, all of whom gave this once-struggling grad student great advice. Edward Linenthal contributed invaluable comments, not to mention some very hard to find sources. In Madison, J. Paul O'Keefe, Brandi Rogers, Chad Goolbis, Cassandra Carlson, and Eric Dienstfrey were a constant source of encouragement—and at times much needed distraction. At the University of Massachusetts Press, special thanks to Clark Dougan for easing me into this project and to Matt Becker for seeing it through.

Then there's the money: fellowships from the Contemporary History Institute made research for this project possible, as did the travel funds provided by Ohio University and Finlandia University. During my visits to the Reagan Presidential Library in 2011, Shelly Nayak was an ideal archivist. Thanks to help of John Lynch at the Vanderbilt Network News Archives, who has provided an important scholarly resource for years, and to the staff at Cornell Library's Special Collections for tracking down the impossible. My colleagues Lauri Anderson, Carolyn Dekker, Leslie Johnson, Mark Lounibos, and Casey Rentmeester all helped in important ways; so did Nathan Bean, Juan Jimenez, David Pagels, and Bob Mackey. To my family: Cheryl and Tim Hicks, Jill Compton, Jane Cameron, A. Abby Knoblauch, and Brian Johnson, deep thanks for all your support over the years. Finally, to Anna Seidel-Quast: I could not have done it, any of it, without you.

NUCLEAR FREEZE IN A COLD WAR

Introduction

The March 29, 1982, cover of *Time* featured an alarming image: a billowing mushroom cloud with a sinister face. *Time*'s headline story, "Thinking about the Unthinkable," reflected the rising levels of nuclear fear in America. Its author, James Kelly, noted that as of that month "from the halls of Congress to Vermont hamlets to the posh living rooms of Beverly Hills, Americans are not only thinking about the unthinkable, they are opening a national dialog on ways to control and reduce the awesome and frightening nuclear arsenals of the superpowers." It was an apt summary of a diverse and growing antinuclear movement. In Congress, Senators Edward Kennedy (D-MA) and Mark Hatfield (R-OR) expressed bipartisan support for a freeze resolution. In Beverly Hills, liberal entertainers, including Blythe Danner and Paul Newman, personally supported and publicly promoted the disarmament cause. Around the nation, grassroots antinuclear protest was at a new high, with numerous groups reengaging in activism. *Time*'s story, therefore, was prescient; in the early 1980s, Americans' nuclear fear was palpable.[1]

Why then, after thirty-five years of living with "the bomb," were Americans again growing so alarmed at the threat of atomic weapons? Nuclear fears had been on the rise since 1979. That March, a reactor accident at Pennsylvania's Three Mile Island (TMI) reminded people of the dangers of nuclear energy, as did *The China Syndrome,* a film serendipitously released only two weeks after TMI which depicted an eerily similar chain of events.[2] Then in July, a massive uranium spill near Church Rock, New Mexico, contaminated the nearby Puerco River. For Americans hoping that nuclear power might provide salvation from the ongoing energy crisis, these sobering events brought home the dangers of atomic energy.

1

Geopolitical events of 1979 also contributed to the rise of nuclear fear. The Iranian Revolution was under way, leading to the overthrow of Mohammad Reza Shah Pahlavi and installing the radical Shi'a cleric Ayatollah Khomeini. Fearing that this radical revolution would spread, and in an action that alarmed the world, in December the Soviet Union invaded Afghanistan, prompting President Jimmy Carter to halt technological exchanges with the Soviets, withdraw the US Olympic team from the 1980 summer games in Moscow, and remove the second Strategic Arms Limitation Treaty (SALT II) from Senate consideration. The era of détente, or relaxation of tensions and acceptance of coexistence with the Soviet Union, was over. Carter called the Soviet invasion the greatest threat to world peace since World War II and proclaimed in his "Carter Doctrine" that any Soviet attempt to control the oil-rich Persian Gulf region would be considered a threat to vital US interests. Carter also agreed to calls by NATO to deploy Pershing II intermediate-range ballistic missiles across Western Europe to counterbalance Soviet SS-20 Saber IRBMs now lining the Eastern Bloc. As the 1970s came to a close, the Cold War seemed to be heating up.[3]

These unsettling events helped pave the way for presidential hopeful Ronald Reagan. A former actor and two-term governor of California, Reagan was a hardline anticommunist who believed that most of the world's ills were the result of Soviet designs. Had the Soviet Union not been "engaged in this game of dominoes," he once remarked, "there wouldn't be any hot spots in the world." Reagan firmly believed that communists were willing "to commit any crime, to lie, to cheat" to achieve world domination.[4] Such rhetoric stood in stark opposition to the Nixon and Ford administrations, which pursued détente through a combination of trade packages and arms reduction treaties with the Soviets. Critics saw these treaties as harmful; so did Reagan, who rejected détente outright. In a 1970s radio address, he once quipped: "Détente . . . isn't that what a farmer has with his turkey until Thanksgiving?" To Reagan, détente was a "one-way street" that favored communism. On the campaign trail, he promised to regain America's Cold War military superiority: "I've called for whatever it takes to be so strong that no other nation will dare violate the peace."[5] The political scientist Beth Fischer has called Reagan's administration "the most vehemently anticommunist administration in U.S. history," while the preeminent Cold War historian John Lewis Gaddis concluded that Reagan "could condemn the Soviet leaders with sincerity and zeal . . . using the harshest rhetoric ever heard from a U.S. President." It was this kind of rhetoric that appealed to many Americans rattled after the geo-political events of 1979 and that helped propel Reagan into office.[6]

Once in office, Reagan's advisers and supporters became bellicose, even brazen, when it came to talk of nuclear war—ever a possibility during the Cold War. Vice President George H. W. Bush boasted of America's ability to "win" a nuclear war, while Defense Secretary Caspar Weinberger pursued a capability not just for deterring but for "prosecuting a global war with the Soviet Union." Deputy Defense Secretary Frank Carlucci III told the Senate that he was seeking a "nuclear-war-fighting capability," while Louis O. Giuffrida, Reagan's head of the Federal Emergency Management Agency (FEMA), commented to ABC News that nuclear war "would be a terrible mess, but it wouldn't be unmanageable." Charles Kupperman, an appointee to the Arms Control and Disarmament Agency, maintained that "it is possible for any society to survive" a nuclear war, while the conservative pundit Colin S. Gray proposed in *Foreign Policy* that when it comes to nuclear war "Victory Is Possible." Perhaps most alarming were the comments of Deputy Under Secretary of Defense T. K. Jones, who offered that "with enough shovels," Americans could survive a nuclear war; all they needed to do was "dig a hole, cover it with a couple of doors and then throw three feet of dirt on top" and citizens would be safe from radioactivity. "It's the dirt that does it . . . if there are enough shovels to go around, everybody's going to make it."[7]

These kinds of remarks not only hinted at a heightened new era of Cold War aggression, they also played on Americans' long-standing fascination with the apocalypse. From the nation's inception, from the Puritan landing, throughout numerous deadly wars, and at every turn of the century, prophecies of the end of time emerged in American culture. Such fears intensified during the Cold War, and understandably so; it was an era of increasingly powerful thermonuclear weapons. The New Testament had long warned of an apocalypse of fire and brimstone, and atomic weapons held the promise to turn prophecy into reality. In the 1940s, religious writers made connections between God's fiery destruction of Sodom and Gomorrah and the arms race, such as Wilbur M. Smith's 1948 book *This Atomic Age and the Word of God*. Secular writers made similar connections. Harvard historian Perry Miller's 1950 essay "The End of the World" noted that atomic destruction sounded similar to millennial apocalyptic prophecies. Throughout the 1950s and early 1960s, as the arms race intensified, numerous works comparing religious and atomic Armageddon manifested.[8] Arguably, the most popular of these works was Hal Lindsey's *The Late Great Planet Earth*. Released in 1970, it argued that biblical end-time prophesies had become all too plausible in the atomic age and became the best-selling "nonfiction" work of the decade. Numerous imitators followed. In the 1980s Doug Clark's *Shockwaves of Armageddon* (1982), Jack Van Impe's *11:59 and Counting* (1983), and S. Maxwell Coder's *The Final Chapter* (1984) made similar connections; so did evangelists like Jerry Falwell.[9] In 1980, Falwell published *Armageddon and the Coming War with Russia,* and by 1983 he aired a radio program titled *Nuclear War and the Second Coming of Jesus Christ.* In the early 1980s, top-ranking administration officials, authors, and evangelists all saw thermonuclear war as a harbinger of biblical apocalypse.[10]

As predictions of the apocalypse grew, so did American interest in nuclear "survivalism." Early Cold War do-it-yourself civil defense, epitomized in the 1950s with the backyard bomb shelter, had waned after the 1962 Cuban missile crisis but returned in a big way in the early 1980s. At California's SI Incorporated and Pennsylvania's Nuclear Fallout and Bombshelter Supply and Construction Company, alongside a selection of "radiation meters, radiation-resistant clothing, anti-contamination kits," customers could purchase *Fallout Survival, Survive the Coming Nuclear War, Life after Doomsday,* and *Nuclear War Survival Skills,* all aimed at Americans "serious about survival . . . especially if you feel that nuclear war is a growing possibility." The advice these books provided may not have always seemed serious— *The Nuclear Survival Handbook* suggested training pet ferrets to catch wild game in the radioactive wasteland—but they did hint at a growing belief that nuclear war could happen.[11]

What made the apocalypse seem possible in the 1980s wasn't just the existence of nuclear weapons—those had been around since 1945; instead it was the individuals Reagan appointed to high office, figures who seemed willing to use these weapons, that frightened the public. Many were disillusioned Democrats and policy intellectuals who in the 1970s had rejected détente; these Neoconservatives sought a return to an aggressive foreign policy reminiscent of the early Cold War.[12] Like Reagan, they saw détente as naïve. Some went a step further, and argued that Central Intelligence Agency estimates of Soviet strength were far too weak. In November 1975, then–CIA director George H. W. Bush allowed a group of Neocons to challenge CIA estimates. Christened "Team B," this group included Edward Teller, the so-called Father of the Hydrogen Bomb and proponent of all things atomic; the Harvard historian Richard Pipes, who believed that the Soviets still pursued global domination; and Paul Nitze, who had helped to draft National Security Council Report-68 (NSC-68), the guiding foreign policy document that outlined containment—America's Cold War strategy that promised to check Soviet expansion anywhere in the world. To check Soviet expansion, Team B proposed an aggressive nuclear arms buildup.[13]

Another influential Neocon organization was the reformed Committee on the Present Danger. Modeled after a 1950s anticommunist group, the 1970s CPD had been busy publishing articles warning policymakers of the growing Soviet threat. For instance, in his essay "Why the Soviet Union Thinks It Could Fight and Win a Nuclear War," Pipes argued that the Soviet Union pursued capabilities to "absorb an American first strike and then retaliate with an overwhelming force."[14] Such dire predictions found a receptive home in conservative journals such as *Commentary*. By the mid-1970s, Reagan was a leading member of the CPD and as president, he appointed thirty-one CPD and Team B members to his administration, including Jeane Kirkpatrick (UN ambassador), William Casey (CIA director), Eugene Rostow (Arms Control and Disarmament Agency director), Richard Pipes (NSC adviser), and Richard Allen (national security adviser).[15] With Reagan's election in 1980, Neocons who had been critically writing about US foreign policy would now be shaping it.

Once in office, the Reagan administration made good on its rhetoric, overseeing the largest peacetime arms buildup in American history. For Reagan, who is often remembered as a fiscal conservative, when it came to defense, the budget was not a consideration. "You spend what you need," he argued, and in the 1980s defense spending increased annually, from $158 billion in fiscal year 1981 to a peak of $304 billion for fiscal year 1989—a total of $2.7 trillion spent on defense. Some of these funds went toward the development of new nuclear weapons and delivery systems, including the B-1 and a new B-2 bomber, the controversial "Missile Experimental" (or MX missiles), Trident missile submarines, intermediate-range cruise missiles, and a reevaluation of nationwide nuclear civil defense plans. This buildup led some Americans to believe that the country was gearing up for nuclear war, and fears were on the rise.[16] The historian George C. Herring has assessed Reagan's first term as a period when "the Cold War re-escalated to a level of tension not equaled since the Cuban missile crisis."[17] Polling data confirm that by the end of 1981, 47 percent of Americans believed that nuclear war was possible; by 1983 close to half of all Americans still believed that they might die in a nuclear war.[18]

For many concerned citizens, this combination of brazen rhetoric and an aggressive arms buildup was too much. Long-dormant antinuclear groups such as the Committee for a Sane Nuclear Policy (SANE), Physicians for Social Responsibility (PSR), and the Union of Concerned Scientists (UCS) saw spikes in membership, and new antinuclear organizations emerged from diverse walks of life, such as the Architects for Social Responsibility, Business Executives Move, Dancers for Disarmament, Life Insurance Industry Committee for a Nuclear Weapons Freeze, Parenting in a Nuclear Age, Performing Artists for Nuclear Disarmament, and Social Workers for Nuclear Disarmament.[19] Clearly, this was not just activism by "radical kooks" or "peaceniks," but a broad coalition of citizens.[20] To SANE's David Cortright, after the 1960s such a coalition was necessary: "In the late 60s and early 70s the peace movement had an aura of anti-patriotism. Our vision is more specific, and we're willing to work with the system, rather than working to bring it down." Cortright concluded: "Now we are in the mainstream—no longer dominated by the student hippie types but rather more by the middle class, religious groups, and women." Helen Caldicott, who served as president of PSR, confirmed that the early 1980s American antinuclear movement was made up of "millions of people across the country arranged in disparate and individual units—churches, psychologists, lawyers, real estate brokers, artists . . . and many more."[21] This broad-based strategy worked. Caldicott gained public support from President Reagan's daughter Patti Davis, SANE's membership grew by 800 percent during Reagan's first term, and by 1983 a nationwide survey showed that "70 percent of all Americans wanted a negotiated freeze on nuclear weapons."[22]

That nuclear "freeze" was the brainchild of Randall Forsberg, a defense researcher and director of the Institute for Defense and Disarmament Studies who in the late 1960s worked for the Stockholm International Peace Institute. Since 1975, she had been pursuing graduate work at MIT and was speaking about nuclear disarmament to a variety of peace groups, all with slightly different agendas and memberships of different socioeconomic and religious backgrounds. Forsberg's breakthrough came with her pamphlet *A Call to Halt the Arms Race,* a plea to stop the "testing, production and deployment of nuclear weapons." The freeze's appeal was in its simplicity; Forsberg had sidestepped the complexities of nuclear defense strategy and appealed to common sense.[23] To date, atomic debates had been dominated by atomic jargon, an alphabet soup of acronyms (ICBMs, MIRVs, SLBMs) and complicated game theory strategies. Forsberg had provided an alternative, one she hoped would make the freeze a "household word," and a "clear alternative to the continuing arms race." Throughout 1982, in towns, cities, and states across the country, the freeze movement grew. On June 12, 1982, an estimated one million Americans flooded the streets of New York City to show their support for the nuclear freeze—the largest antinuclear rally in American history; by November, freeze referenda were set to appear on ten state ballots. Forsberg had achieved a broad base of support.[24]

This level of antinuclear activism had not been seen since the immediate postwar years, a period captured in Paul S. Boyer's *By the Bomb's Early Light*. In this pathbreaking work, Boyer discerned stages of American "nuclear consciousness" to show that from 1945 until 1950, US citizens experienced a cycle of "heightened fear, activism, and cultural attention to the bomb" that ultimately "gave way with surprising suddenness to intervals when the nuclear reality seemed to sink out of sight." This cycle was not identifiable through archival research or digging through official government documents; only through a close reading of popular culture could scholars accurately assess America's evolving relationship with "the bomb." When Boyer began research for *By the Bomb's Early Light* in 1981, he encountered "profound public apathy towards the threat of nuclear war."[25] Shortly after Reagan was elected, however, this "climate changed," and "the stage was already set for a return to the oldest item on the agenda: the threat of nuclear war." The combination of Reagan's "bellicose rhetoric, his vast military buildup, his elaborate and heavily publicized civil-defense programs, his proposals to push the nuclear arms race into space, and the barely concealed contempt of powerful administration figures for the whole concept of arms control" led to a renewal of "antinuclear activism and revived cultural awareness."[26] "In a curious way," Boyer later reflected, "America's nuclear history in the early 1980s recapitulated early postwar patterns of opinion and manipulation."[27]

This is the story of those renewed patterns of opinion and manipulation in the early 1980s, not from the perspective of grassroots activists, but from two distinct groups who battled over public perception of the nuclear threat. The first is the Reagan administration, specifically those officials in charge of communications and public relations, and especially the cabinet members who worked to maintain public support in a period of heightened atomic anxiety. The second group includes the authors, publishers, directors, musicians, and celebrities who actively critiqued Reagan's arms race. I have labeled this latter group "antinuclear cultural activists," a term that demands some definition. These individuals did more than express political convictions in art; rather, these were activists who—using their privileged access to print and digital media in a pre-Internet age—created meaningful and effective pieces of propaganda with the potential to sway public opinion. When their efforts began transforming apathy into activism, the Reagan administration responded.

In examining this battle, I have framed a simple thesis: Throughout the early 1980s, antinuclear cultural activists threatened Reagan's arms buildup. A combination of archival research, cultural analysis, and interviews reveal that these activists' efforts to support the freeze had short-term success, but in the long term they provided the White House with opportunities to reshape Reagan's image and publicize their new foreign policy initiatives. They did this by adeptly co-opting the rhetoric of the nuclear freeze campaign in American mass media.

Who were these antinuclear cultural activists? They include the author Jonathan Schell, whose 1982 work *The Fate of the Earth* reached the *New York Times* best-seller list; Roger Molander, a former NSC staffer under Presidents Nixon, Ford, and Carter who wrote *Nuclear War: What's in It for You?*, a paperback that made national headlines and coordinated cross-country antinuclear campus protests and sit-ins; the director Nicholas Meyer, whose film *The Day After* earned record ratings and prompted nationwide debate on nuclear weapons; and the celebrity scientist Carl Sagan, who promoted the "nuclear winter" hypothesis in popular magazines, in newspapers, and on television. The archives reveal that the White House recognized the potential of cultural activism to influence millions of Americans into joining the antinuclear cause, and in response the Reagan administration worked to contain these efforts.

In the pages that follow, President Reagan and his top-ranking officials— such as Secretary of State George Shultz, Defense Secretary Weinberger, and Vice President Bush—all make appearances, but they are not the primary actors in this story. Instead, it is the lesser-known figures, the men and women who planned and implemented public relations campaigns, who play the most prominent roles. After all, this was the administration that created the Office of Media Relations, then led by Karna Small-Stringer, who worked closely with Assistant to the President for National Security Affairs William Clark, Assistant to the President for Communications David Gergen, Special Assistant to the Chief of Staff James Cicconi, and Counsel to the President Fred Fielding. These figures were instrumental in containing antinuclear cultural activism and regaining the public's support.

Because so many of these media battles coincided, a strictly chronological approach becomes problematic. For instance, Carl Sagan began a prolonged media campaign to discredit Reagan's Strategic Defense Initiative in March 1983, while in October he embarked on an ambitious campaign to spread warnings of a nuclear winter, and in November he promoted that theory after the airing of the film *The Day After*. Similar overlaps occurred with Reagan administration efforts. David Gergen, for example, worked on media campaigns to contain the popularity of the nuclear freeze in 1982, minimize backlash from *The Day After* in 1983, and rebrand SDI in 1985. Because of such overlaps, chapters are organized thematically, although they are ordered chronologically according to the time period in which activists and the Reagan administration were most engaged in a particular media battle.

Those battles began in March 1982, a month in which antinuclear literature topped best-seller lists. Chapter 1 traces the efforts of authors and publishers who sacrificed profits in favor of a wide readership that fueled the nuclear freeze campaign. To combat their efforts, the Reagan administration engaged its "Peaceful Offensive," a sprawling media campaign to co-opt freeze rhetoric. Chapter 2 traces Carl Sagan's efforts to promote a new vision of atomic apocalypse—the "nuclear winter"—and how the National Security Council and the Defense Department worked to discredit Sagan personally. Chapter 3 explores the White House's coordinated efforts to turn the media frenzy surrounding the film *The Day After* into an opportunity to pivot their hardline message. Reagan's controversial Strategic Defense Initiative is the focus of chapter 4, specifically the battle between two nongovernmental organizations, High Frontier and the Union of Concerned Scientists, which created propaganda that delineated public perceptions of "Star Wars" and left the Reagan administration scrambling to control SDI debates.

Examining these battles between administration officials and antinuclear cultural activists complicates previous assessments of antinuclear culture and its effectiveness in promoting the freeze campaign. Such conclusions often came from pundits who relied on polling data from the 1980s. Consider *The Day After*, one of the most widely watched media events of the decade. Polls taken shortly after it aired concluded that the film did little to sway Americans' opinions about nuclear war; similarly, regarding the promotion of nuclear winter, two biographers have been critical of Sagan's seeming inability to enact meaningful policy changes. Such criticisms of 1980s antinuclear activism fail to capture the whole story, however. White House documents, many recently declassified, reveal that the Reagan administration took these efforts seriously. What follows, then, is not a story of winners and losers in the struggle over nuclear proliferation. Instead, this is book about battles over public opinion by two groups, who each believed they were on the right side of history. Antinuclear cultural activists saw atomic salvation in the freeze, while administration officials were convinced in the importance of an overwhelming deterrent.

A final note to the reader: in my research, I never discovered any concrete "reversal" of Reagan's thinking, any clear "rebellion" against his cabinet, or any flashpoint event that radically changed Reagan's mind. What I did discover was a gradual transition within the administration, one influenced by a growing imperative to contain antinuclear propaganda. The numerous challenges these cultural activists posed actually helped the White House during a period in which pragmatists slowly assumed control of policy and began to pursue a posture of peace. Even if they never achieved the kind of immediate nuclear freeze they desired, the efforts of these activists were far from ineffectual.

1

Fear Books

The March 26, 1982, issue of *Publishers Weekly* featured "A Checklist of Nuclear Books" which included a timely question from the editor Joann Davis: "Fear books. Books that deliver disquieting messages about radiation leaks and environmental poisons and bombs so powerful they could ultimately destroy the human race. Most of us have a hard time escaping these horrors on the nightly news and in the morning papers. Do we really want to read about them in our leisure time?"[1] If the *New York Times* best-seller list was any indication, the answer to Davis's question was yes. In response to the Reagan administration's rhetoric and arms buildup, antinuclear nonfiction—defined here as any bound nonfiction work in print that was critical of nuclear weapons—sold relatively well in early 1982.[2]

This new crop of antinuclear nonfiction was a result of rising fears largely fueled by the Reagan administration's tough talk supporting its arms buildup. In time, the growing popularity of these books led the White House to consider that perhaps it had gone too far with its brazen rhetoric. As the journalist Robert Scheer assessed, "By the spring of 1982, the Administration realized that it had got itself into deep trouble on this issue [nuclear war] and began to alter its public posture."[3] That analysis is certainly correct; however, Scheer's account overlooks the important role that writers and publishers of antinuclear paperbacks played in this turnabout. In the early 1980s, an increasing number of antinuclear nonfiction books rallied Americans to the disarmament cause and helped to galvanize huge protests.

To put this phenomenon in context, consider the April 12, 1982, *Newsweek* article "The Nuclear Book Boom," which noted that between 1979 and 1983 more than 130 antinuclear books entered the literary marketplace. After months of Reagan administration rhetoric about "winning" or "prevailing" in a nuclear war, publishers anticipated "a brisk business" for books critical of the arms race. It was a rare prediction for a Cold War literary subgenre that historically sold modestly; Joann Davis remarked that "even taking into account publishers' habitual consignment of slow-selling titles—and books about nuclear matters often fall into this category—this statistic still indicates considerable growth."[4] This flood of antinuclear paperbacks wasn't fueled by profit but by publishers' political convictions. Daniel Moses of Sierra Club Books commented that "editors and publishers don't expect to sell a lot of books on [nuclear war]. It's not a commercial enterprise. I think they genuinely feel an obligation to inform the public on this issue."[5] In other words, early 1980s publishers who put antinuclear paperbacks into the marketplace despite traditionally low sales figures were engaging in a form of antinuclear activism.

Of these 130 paperbacks, four in particular led to the Reagan administration's media response. The first, *The Unforgettable Fire*, predated Reagan's presidency but it proved to publishers that readers were again interested in antinuclear literature. The second, Jonathan Schell's *The Fate of the Earth*, warned about the dangers of the arms race in vivid detail. When Schell's book topped best-seller lists, it inspired *Nuclear War: What's in It for You?*, a book by the antinuclear group Ground Zero that became an important promotional and organizational tool for a nationwide "Ground Zero Week." Finally, recognizing the political impact of these books, Senators Edward Kennedy and Mark Hatfield published *Freeze!: How You Can Help Prevent Nuclear War*, which aimed to build support for upcoming freeze resolutions to appear in midterm elections in ten states. The seriousness with which the Reagan administration responded to this nuclear book boom confirms antinuclear nonfiction's potential to bolster the freeze movement.

The Unforgettable Fire

Lawrence Wittner, a scholar of the antinuclear movement, notes that "during the early 1970s, nuclear weapons went largely unnoticed" in American activist circles, and that "in contrast to earlier upsurges of public concern and antinuclear activism . . . there was relatively little popular protest against nuclear weapons in the 1970s." The historian Paul Boyer concurs, calling this period the "Big Sleep," or the "period of diminished attention to nuclear issues that extended from 1963 to the later 1970s."[6] Even as nuclear proliferation became a global issue, in the 1970s American antinuclear activism was, by comparison to the 1950s or early 1980s, moderate. That began to change on March 29, 1979, when a meltdown nearly occurred at Three Mile Island nuclear power plant. The accident resulted from a combination of engineer negligence, faulty control panel gauges, and reactor relief valve disruption. Although engineers prevented a total reactor failure, the radioactive steam released contaminated the surrounding community and nearby Susquehanna River. TMI made headlines just as the major motion picture *The China Syndrome*—featuring a story of events remarkably like the Pennsylvania nuclear accident—hit the theaters. Together, TMI and *The China Syndrome* reenergized nuclear power debates.[7]

Three Mile Island also influenced the publication of *The Unforgettable Fire*, a project initiated by the editor and writer Tom Engelhardt. Immediately after TMI, Engelhardt met with Ann Marie Cunningham, a member of President Carter's Commission on the Accident at Three Mile Island, who related a story. After the accident, Japanese reporters traveled to Pennsylvania to interview locals, including displaced expecting mothers; as a safety precaution, these women had been relocated from their homes to an abandoned skating rink in Harrisburg. Questioning the women about fears of radioactivity and their knowledge of Hiroshima, one reporter was alarmed to discover that only a few of the dozens of women interviewed knew anything about the US atomic bombings of Japan.[8]

The story shocked Engelhardt. As a child, the film *Hiroshima Mon Amour* made a lasting impression on him, especially its images of Hiroshima survivors, while living through the 1962 Cuban missile crisis solidified his fear of nuclear weapons. Like many young Americans in the 1960s, Engelhardt protested the Vietnam War, and he remained politically active afterward. Cunningham's story redirected his activism to the antinuclear movement. He decided to publish a book about Hiroshima, and asked a friend, the historian John Dower, for advice. Dower first suggested publishing a collection of photographs taken in Hiroshima after the bombings, but these images proved "too grim" for public consumption; then, he sent Engelhardt a collection of pastels and drawings by Hiroshima survivors titled *The Unforgettable Fire*. Engelhardt was moved, and convinced Pantheon Books to publish the collection in the United States.[9]

The original Japanese publication of *The Unforgettable Fire* predates its US release by six years. The project began in 1974 when a Hiroshima survivor, Iwakichi Kobayashi, entered the Hiroshima NHK television studios. Inspired by a recent program on the bomb's survivors, Kobayashi shared his own sketch, drawn from memory, with the company's producers. Awestruck by the "extraordinary power of Mr. Kobayashi's picture and the vividness of his memory even after almost thirty years," NHK put out a call for Hiroshima survivors to submit atomic bomb drawings and received numerous submissions from amateur artists forever scarred by the bomb.[10] These images were featured in an NHK program commemorating the thirtieth anniversary of the bombings and later comprised the moving display at the Peace Culture Center in Hiroshima City.

Engelhardt recalls the impact these unsettling images had on American readers: "In America . . . in the mainstream . . . there had never been a book that went under the mushroom cloud. You could look at the ruins, but you couldn't see . . . the human beings. If you were on the fringes and you knew comics, if you knew *Barefoot Gen* . . . maybe . . . but there wasn't much." Engelhardt believes that *The Unforgettable Fire* became a sensation because it provided the "first full-scale publication of the memories of survivors of Hiroshima since John Hersey." Hersey, author of the 1946 work *Hiroshima*, agreed. He found the book to be "tremendously moving—more moving than any book of photographs of the horror could be, because what is registered is what has been burned into the minds of the survivors." Many in the American news media echoed these sentiments. A *New York Times* reviewer, for example, argued that *The Unforgettable Fire* "deserves a place next to John Hersey's *Hiroshima*."[11]

As Reagan administration rhetoric about winning a nuclear war intensified, *The Unforgettable Fire* became a political tool, a book that came to represent not the past, but the potential future horrors of what awaited survivors of a nuclear war. "The book became an integral part [of] the antinuclear weapons movement," recalls Engelhardt, and these images were used in an exhibit at the Chicago Peace Museum.[12] Mark Rogovin, curator and museum cofounder, recalled that *The Unforgettable Fire* contained "the most powerful visual documents [he] had ever seen" regarding atomic weapons, and the exhibit ran for close to a year. On November 30, 1982, Rogovin took these images on the road, touring America with a mobile exhibit and prompting newspapers to report on the "powerful effect" *The Unforgettable Fire* had on citizens who realized for the first time "just how dreadful it was for the people [attacked]."[13] The exhibit even influenced the Irish rock group U2 to write a song and title their politically charged 1984 album *The Unforgettable Fire*.[14]

Engelhardt's collection, then, hinted to writers and publishers that serious antinuclear books could have an impact. One writer even appropriated excerpts from *The Unforgettable Fire* for his forthcoming series of essays set to appear in the *New Yorker*. That writer was Jonathan Schell, and his series, *The Fate of the Earth*, would become one of the most popular antinuclear publications in US history.

The Fate of the Earth

The Fate of the Earth began as a three-part serialized essay that could convey the horrific details of nuclear war in accessible language. Schell had devoted five years to the project, researching the consequences of nuclear war by interviewing biologists, ecologists, and weapons experts, all of which lent Schell's arguments more than an air of expertise. Still, his plain but illustrative prose helped to assure a wide readership. Plausible, unflinching, and frightening, Schell's *The Fate of the Earth* quickly became required reading for Americans in, or interested in joining, the rapidly growing antinuclear movement.[15]

In early 1982, when *The Fate of the Earth* first appeared in the *New Yorker*, antinuclear grassroots activism was already on the rise, a trend evidenced by the growth of the Randall Forsberg–led nuclear freeze campaign. Forsberg recognized the role of literature in building a broad coalition from the American middle class, a lesson learned from her time protesting the Vietnam War. She grasped *The Fate of the Earth*'s importance, and by promoting the book she hoped to ensure that it became a must-read for freeze activists.[16] Additionally, Schell's ability to sidestep the authority of nuclear strategists, those mathematicians and economists who had long held prominence in nuclear debates—the men Fred Kaplan called the "Wizards of Armageddon"—meant that *The Fate of the Earth* held the potential to reach nonactivists and convert them to the antinuclear cause.[17]

In explaining the realities of the atomic age, Schell was blunt. Nuclear war wouldn't really be war at all, but human extinction. Governments were lying; in fact, they had been in denial about atomic dangers for some thirty-seven years. Survivalism was futile, and the nuclear threat was far greater than anticipated. During and after a nuclear war, death would come in many forms: gamma rays, blast waves, fallout, and, after stripping the ozone, sunburn. It would mean certain death not only for humans, but for animals and plant life, which would lead to widespread human starvation. Nuclear war, then, would not just kill one generation, but doom all future generations. Faced with potential extinction, the only way for humanity to proceed was to grapple with the nuclear threat head-on; for Schell, that meant international control of the bomb—a solution that required a rethinking of nation-state atomic autonomy in the pursuit of global disarmament.[18]

The Fate of the Earth's most graphic section may be "A Republic of Insects and Grass," which examines the ecological, biological, and societal consequences of a nuclear war. Schell argues that lessons from history, and in particular the US atomic bombing of Japan, could only show Americans a fraction of the devastation that awaited them in a modern, full-scale nuclear war. Here, he appropriates quotes and imagery from *The Unforgettable Fire* to narrate the horrors that awaited Hiroshima's survivors:

> In the weeks after the bombing, many survivors began to notice the appearance of petechiae—small spots caused by hemorrhages—on their skin. These usually signaled the onset of the critical stage of radiation sickness. In the first stage, the victims characteristically vomited repeatedly, ran a fever, and developed an abnormal thirst. (The cry "Water! Water!" was one of the few sounds often heard in Hiroshima on the day of the bombing.) Then, after a few hours or days, there was a deceptively hopeful period of remission of symptoms, called the latency period, which lasted from about a week to about four weeks . . . in the third, and final, stage . . . the victim's hair may fall out and he may suffer from diarrhea and may bleed from the intestines, the mouth, or other parts of the body, and in the end he will either recover or die.[19]

It's a haunting passage, one of many. Schell provided readers with much disturbing imagery, such as, "The naked man, standing on the blasted plain that was his city, holding his eyeball in his hand." The Japanese experience after Hiroshima, then, shows the inability of a government to deal with a nuclear attack, and atomic bombs of 1945 were comparably weak; modern thermonuclear weapons, Schell assures us, would lead to even worse consequences: "In the months after a holocaust, there would be no activity of any sort, as, in a reversal of the normal state of things, the dead would lie on the surface and the living, if there were any, would be buried underground."[20] For readers in 1982, the message was clear: despite recent rhetoric of administration officials, no government—and no amount of shovels—could provide immediate action or relief from the horrors of nuclear holocaust.

Between its initial appearance in the *New Yorker* on February 1, 1982, to its release as a book in April 1982, Jonathan Schell deliberated how best to distribute *The Fate of the Earth*. His decision on the book's format and price mattered, as publishers considered their demographics carefully when choosing these factors. There were three common format options: hardcover, mass-market paperbacks, and trade paperbacks. Hardcovers had the highest profit margins, while trade paperbacks were more cost-effective and were a popular choice for second printings; mass-market paperbacks, however, were the cheapest to produce, making it the default format of pop romances and pulp fiction. Publishers uncertain of a book's success often chose the mass-market paperback to minimize potential loss, and settled on the larger and more alluring trade paperback format for books likely to sell, usually second runs of hardcovers. This was a format aimed at affluent readers who might proudly display these works on their bookshelves.[21]

In February 1982, the substantial buzz surrounding *The Fate of the Earth* almost ensured that once it became a book, it would be a best seller. If Schell and Knopf, his publisher, only sought profits, they would have stuck with the traditional hardcover format; instead, Schell preferred mass-market paperback—the most cost-effective medium. Schell's choice was intentional; he wanted to spread an antinuclear message to the greatest number of readers. In another step that sacrificed profits for readership, Knopf's hardcover $11.95 price tag was lower than expected, and it later offered the *The Fate of the Earth* paperback at cost.[22] So did the Book of the Month Club (BOMC), whose editor-in-chief Gloria Norris explained "[We made] a special effort to bring [*The Fate of the Earth*] to people's attention." Knopf's editor-in-chief Robert Gottlieb also preferred publicity over profits: "My main interest is that the world not nuke itself, not that we sell a lot of copies." Schell, then, made an "unusual agreement" with publishers so as to receive only a minimum royalty for sales. By April 1982, Book of the Month Club's 1.2 million subscribers could purchase *The Fate of the Earth* for only $2.25 a copy. It was a low-cost, high-readership strategy that worked. Knopf quickly sold out, and had to increase its original print order from 35,000 to 75,000 copies.[23]

As sales skyrocketed, the book made headlines. The *CBS Evening News,* the *New York Times,* and the *Wall Street Journal* reviewed the book favorably; even the *Merv Griffin Show* mentioned *The Fate of the Earth*. On CBS television's *Face the Nation,* presidential hopeful Walter Mondale called Schell's writings "historic." Soon, *The Fate of the Earth* was on the *New York Times* best-seller list. This meteoric rise to cultural prominence led one critic to call Schell's book "a remarkable achievement." Noting the media frenzy that followed *The Fate of the Earth*'s publication, the *Washington Post* commented that from antinuclear activists to novelists and politicians, "Jonathan Schell's *The Fate of the Earth* has people talking."[24]

Politicians quickly recognized the book's power and courted Schell's support. Senator Alan Cranston (D-CA), who accepted Schell's "thesis that all-out nuclear war could mean the end of the human race," traveled to New York City to meet the author and ask him to summarize his book for distribution in Congress. The political commentator Bill Moyers said that *The Fate of the Earth* "seems destined to be one of the small number of books which occasionally play a great part in opening the public mind to dimly perceived truths." PSR leader Helen Caldicott called Schell's book "the new Bible of our time, the White Paper of our age," and it became required reading for PSR activists.[25] On television, Mondale expressed his belief that Schell's book should become "mandatory reading," while Senator Kennedy entered "A Republic of Insects and Grass" into the *Congressional Record*. Concerned scientists even used *The Fate of the Earth* to drive home the horrors of nuclear apocalypse to world leaders. For instance, as part of the Vatican's Science Advisory Committee, the former Manhattan Project member and MIT physicist Victor Weisskopf presented a copy of *The Fate of the Earth* to the Pope in hopes of influencing the Catholic leader's views on nuclear war. Schell's book, therefore, held the potential to persuade politicians, protestors, and pontiffs alike.[26]

Then there were the detractors. The conservative-leaning *Wall Street Journal* attacked the *New Yorker* as a "bastion of limousine liberalism" and called Schell's book "destructive of serious thought about how to prevent war and control the spread of nuclear arms." Defense analysts took issue with Schell's predictions of human extinction, citing a National Academy of Sciences study of nuclear war report that concluded "human life would survive even the largest nuclear war." Kurt Guthe, an analyst at the Hudson Institute (a conservative think tank) scoffed at Schell's doom and gloom predictions, and countered that instead "we should be concerned with how best to deter such a war and mitigate the damage if it does occur."[27] Guthe found Schell's call for disarmament "entirely unrealistic, like a freshman paper." Some reviewers critiqued, "Mr. Schell can't be bothered with policy," and argued that while he contemplates an unlikely internationalism and global atomic abolitionism, "the rest of us are left in the real world."[28]

Even if Schell was musing philosophical, many thinkers in the "real world" were taking note. *The Fate of the Earth* had intensified debate over the Reagan administration's arms buildup and "insensitive" foreign policy, and the Cold War establishment responded with new recommendations. McGeorge Bundy, George Kennan, Robert McNamara, and Gerard Smith, a venerable collection of "wise men" in the realm of Cold War nuclear strategy, now recommended that America promote a "never first use" policy when it came to atomic weapons.[29] The public responded as well. In op-eds and editorials nationwide, they debated the merits of Schell's book. One April 22 *New York Times* letter to the editor responded harshly to *The Fate of the Earth*'s critics, especially this distracting fixation on "real world" problems. Such arguments simply missed the point; ideology and geopolitics were not the issue—the issue was nuclear weaponry, which "has now become the enemy." Average Americans needed to heed Schell's call, for "nothing less than our moral survival is at stake." Clearly, *The Fate of the Earth* was rousing impassioned debate, and such editorials show the book's ability to reach and inspire nonactivists.[30]

It was this ability to reach middle America that alarmed the White House. While established antinuclear groups such as the PSR, UCS, and SANE were sure to oppose Reagan's arms buildup, *The Fate of the Earth* was broadening that dissent. Schell's book was "rapidly becoming a guidebook for the antinuclear protestors," and newspaper editorials confirmed that "people who don't read books are reading Jonathan Schell's *The Fate of the Earth,*" a phenomena similar to Rachel Carson's *Silent Spring,* the 1962 book that helped launch the modern environmental movement. Writing in the early 1980s, the historian Paul Boyer saw Schell's book as "enormously influential" in fueling antinuclear activism.[31] *The Fate of the Earth* became a national best seller, and the freeze further grew in popularity; soon, another antinuclear group hoped to mimic Schell's success in awakening activism with an inexpensive paperback. That group was Ground Zero.

Nuclear War: What's in It For You?

By 1980, Robert Molander had grown fearful over the possibility of nuclear war. Trained as a nuclear engineer, Molander had worked his way up the ranks to become a senior staffer in the National Security Council, but he noticed that discussions about using nuclear weapons were increasing.[32] The 1979 Soviet invasion of Afghanistan greatly concerned him, as did Jimmy Carter's Presidential Directive 59, a secret proposal that put limited nuclear strikes on the table, so long as civilian fatalities remained "acceptable." It was a document that Molander saw as a dangerous step closer to nuclear war. "[When] the Russians had invaded Afghanistan . . . I somehow felt that the bell had begun to toll," recalls Molander, "that we had to crack into people's consciousness" about the threat of nuclear weapons.[33] Cracking that consciousness would not be easy; by the early 1980s, the psychologist Robert Jay Lifton had even created a term describing Americans' refusal to grapple with the bomb: "psychic numbing." Sure, Americans knew of the nuclear threat, but they felt helpless in fighting it. Statistics supported Lifton's theory. A Gallup poll from October 5, 1981, concluded that 47 percent of those queried on the possibility of nuclear war responded that they had tried "not to think about the unpleasant question."[34]

To overcome this "psychic numbing," Molander and his twin brother Earl started Ground Zero, a nonpartisan group that could take on the "confusion and frustration the American people experience as they confront [nuclear weapons'] threat to their security." The Molanders ambitiously planned a nationwide event, Ground Zero Week, "a concentrated and nonpartisan educational process on nuclear war, a forum for education, discussion and debate" set for April 18–25, 1982. Seeking a broad base, Ground Zero invited not just peace organizations and universities to participate, but such groups as the United Auto Workers, the Rotary Club, and the American Legion. To promote the event, Molander received $100,000 from various contributors including the Rockefeller Fund; inspired by *The Fate of the Earth*, Molander decided to publish his own antinuclear paperback.[35]

The result was *Nuclear War: What's in It for You?*, a book that served as "the primary educational resource for the activities of Ground Zero Week." Its subjects range from the historical (the dawn of the atomic age, the Cuban missile crisis) to the contemporary (nuclear war scenarios, the environmental consequences of nuclear war), all in accessible language aimed at a wide audience. This emphasis on reaching non-specialists is evident from page one. The book begins with a fictional narrative based on one plausible "wargame" scenario: When Soviet military actions in the Middle East trigger a US response, events spiral out of control, leading to a limited nuclear attack on the United States. Readers follow the plight of a badly burned son and his injured sister, who take refuge in their home miles away from the initial blast site. Without electricity, heat, or substantial supplies, their mother—an army widow—ponders how her family will survive and wonders why she didn't do more to protest.

All the careful talk about nuclear weapons. BOMBS, that's what they were really talking about. BOMBS. *Weapons* is just a nice word . . . like when they used to call them devices. That's what they called them after Hiroshima . . . It was all so abstract, so remote. People simply don't have nuclear wars. Things could never get so out of control. She tried to recall what she had read in the newspapers about nuclear war. All she could remember were the strange names and numbers . . . Should she have read more carefully? Should she have *tried* to understand all the strange names—M-X, B-1, ICBM, SS-18, MIRV, Backfire, Trident? Well, at this point, it didn't seem to matter very much.

Clearly, like *The Fate of the Earth*, *Nuclear War* aimed to transcend the air of expertise from atomic jargon and drive home the horrors of nuclear war.[36]

His nuclear primer written, Molander now needed a major publishing house to reach a mass audience. He contacted Pocket Books and its editor-in-chief, Martin Asher, and asked if Pocket might "devote its expertise in mass-market merchandising" to a book with "a style easily comprehended by the average American" and written in "the Dr. Strangelove mode, with a touch of wry humor."[37] Asher agreed. The editor knew that *The Fate of the Earth* was scheduled for publication, but he assessed Schell's prose as geared toward "liberals and New York sophisticates." Molander's proposal for a plain-language publication for the average middle American was appealing. Like *The Fate of the Earth*'s publishers, Asher pursued the project not for profit, but because of his desire to shape antinuclear debates. "As a father of young children," Asher remarked, "I shared Molander's feelings" about nuclear war.[38]

Pocket Books marketed *Nuclear War* in much the same way that Knopf and BOMC did *The Fate of the Earth*—as a mass-market paperback offered at the cost price of $2.95. The approach worked, and like *The Fate of the Earth*, *Nuclear War* became a best seller. After the first 100,000 copies sold out, Pocket Books ordered a second printing of 125,000 paperbacks; by March 1982, over 225,000 copies flooded the market.[39] Like *The Fate of the Earth*, high sales came with criticism. Some saw *Nuclear War*'s introductory chapter as watered down; the *Washington Post* called it "liberal sentimentalism run amok."[40] Another review criticized *Nuclear War* as a "well-intentioned primer that reduces the complexities of the Manhattan Project during the Second World War and subsequent U.S.-Soviet foreign policy to cartoon scenarios." But even critical reviews promoted the upcoming Ground Zero Week, and soon the event was nationwide news.[41] According to the *Christian Science Monitor*, "Nobody can open up a newspaper or magazine or snap on a television set without, sooner or later, encountering the newly obsessive subject" of nuclear war and Ground Zero Week.[42]

Mass media was flooded with Ground Zero stories. On television, a "Ground Zero" forum at Harvard's John F. Kennedy School of Government featured students feeding questions straight from *Nuclear War* to notable nuclear strategists and statesmen—including Henry Kissinger, Herman Kahn, Edward Teller, and McGeorge Bundy.[43] The *Village Voice* printed Ground Zero Week's "Making Peace Happen: A Calendar for Survival," a schedule of public talks such as "Effects of Nuclear War on Children," and "Nuclear Arms Negotiation: Where Do We Go from Here?" as well as more uplifting events including a "run for your life" marathon and a "dances against death" competition. Molander oversaw the distribution of thousands of pamphlets to promote Ground Zero Week coast to coast. "The threat of nuclear war has never been greater," it read, and only "education and motivation [can] serve as a catalyst for a new consensus building process in this nation on the nuclear war issue." Ground Zero reached 750 communities and 450 college campuses nationwide, with more than a million Americans in over two thousand cities set to participate in Ground Zero Week.[44]

As the buzz for Ground Zero Week reached a fever pitch, politicians took note. In March, Kennedy and Hatfield declared bipartisan support for a freeze resolution in the Senate, one that called for "a mutual and verifiable nuclear weapons freeze." Tennessee representative Albert Gore Jr. provided a detailed plan on how such a moratorium on the arms race could be implemented. After the resolution gained the support of over 190 members of Congress, Kennedy and Hatfield pushed for statewide referendums with similar freeze proposals. Schell's *The Fate of the Earth* and Molander's *Nuclear War* had proved the effectiveness of antinuclear paperbacks in organizing and promoting antinuclear events; perhaps a similar mass-market paperback could build support for congressional freeze proposals. In 1982, Hatfield and Kennedy oversaw the publication of *Freeze! How You Can Help Prevent Nuclear War*, a calculated attempt to piggyback on Ground Zero Week publicity.[45]

Freeze!: How You Can Help Prevent Nuclear War

Freeze! was set into motion on April 2, 1982, after the literary agent Sterling Lord—then representing Senator Kennedy—pushed the idea to Bantam Book editor Linda Grey. Lord believed that if there was a book that coincided with Ground Zero Week, the freeze movement could capitalize on

Molander's publicity efforts; additionally, such a book could be used as a political tool for the upcoming midterm elections. Kennedy and Hatfield agreed and quickly ordered their staffs to rush materials to Bantam, a publishing house with experience producing "instant books," or rapidly written and distributed mass-market paperbacks (such as *The Warren Commission Report* and *The Pentagon Papers*). The turnaround was impressive; Bantam produced and published the paperback in only two weeks. By April 18, 1982, more than 200,000 copies of *Freeze!* adorned bookstore shelves right alongside *Nuclear War* and *The Fate of the Earth*.[46]

Freeze! avoided *Nuclear War*'s fictional narratives and stuck to history and politics. It begins with an account of the Hiroshima bombing and compares it to a hypothetical modern-day attack on New York City which, in a thermonuclear age, would be much more devastating. Later chapters examine the global environmental and biological consequences of nuclear war, the "Illusion of Civil Defense," the necessity of activism in ending the arms race, and a helpful FAQ on the nuclear freeze campaign, including local office addresses and contact information. Clearly, the goal for the book was not simply to inform Americans of the nuclear threat; it was to be a tool that could help pass freeze resolutions—a goal driven home in four appendixes: "The Kennedy-Hatfield Congressional Nuclear Freeze Resolution and Its Supporters"; "Witnesses for a Nuclear Freeze," or brief testimonies from government and religious leaders explaining their support for disarmament; "The Nuclear Freeze Campaign—Names and Addresses"; and contact information for members of Congress.[47]

Perhaps because it was so blatantly a political tool, *Freeze!* received some harsh criticisms. The *Washington Post*'s David Broder attacked *Freeze!* alongside *Nuclear War* for touting bipartisanship but in reality providing "no balanced, factual information." Both books were full of "emotionalism and sentimentalism" when serious nuclear debates should be left to knowledgeable policymakers—for example, Senator Sam Nunn (D-GA) and his recent calls for increased superpower dialogue. Nunn exemplified the "seriousness with which this survival issue needs to be discussed," as evidenced by the lack of "emotionalism in his speeches and writing on this subject."[48] Perhaps these criticisms were warranted, but if the purpose of *Freeze!* was to excite activism, emotionalism helped. The book helped to catalyze the June 12, 1982, New York City Freeze rally. What began as a modest protest organized by the Southern Christian Leadership Conference and the American Friends Service Committee became—in the wake of the best-selling books *The Fate of* the Earth, Nuclear War, and Freeze!—the largest antinuclear demonstration in American history. Freeze activists marched while musicians including Bob Dylan, Joan Baez, Bruce Springsteen, Jackson Browne, and Bonnie Raitt sang in support.[49] Such high-profile participation and sheer numbers led to considerable network news coverage of the event, and disarmament proponents hoped that this momentum would carry into the fall and shape the 1982 midterm elections.

With the economy still in dismal shape, and freeze activism at a fever pitch, the Reagan administration found itself on the defensive. Moreover, antinuclear activism was paying political dividends; the Nuclear Freeze movement was now impossible to ignore, and freeze referendums were appearing on the ballots in thirty-eight cities, nine states, and the District of Columbia.[50] The momentum seemed to be working in the freeze's favor, but by June 1982, the White House had begun to respond. Coordinating their efforts since March when The Fate of the Earth started making headlines, the administration's goal was to co-opt freeze rhetoric in the hopes of stopping freeze referenda that could impede their arms buildup. They called this plan the "Peaceful Offensive."

The White House Responds

In a March 1982 interview, the White House pollster Richard Wirthlin predicted that "peace" would be the big issue of November's midterm elections. That spring, polls showed considerable public support for the nuclear freeze, and if left unchecked that support would only grow through the summer.[51] As Douglas C. Waller points out in Congress and the Nuclear Freeze Campaign, as the midterm elections approached in the fall of 1982 "opinion polls [on the nuclear freeze] consistently showed two-thirds or more of the public supporting the idea," making it "the closest this nation has ever come to a national referendum on the nuclear arms race."[52] The administration knew it had to act, and fast. The centerpiece of their rhetoric would be the recently proposed Strategic Arms Reduction Treaty, or START, a bilateral arms reduction proposal—meaning that unlike unilateral calls for "freeze" by one nation, START necessitated a verifiable builddown by both superpowers.

In the March 21 Sunday Edition of the New York Times, the administration offered START as a step beyond a well-meaning but ultimately dangerous unilateral freeze:

While we understand the spirit that motivates the freeze efforts, the Administration cannot support the freeze itself. It would freeze the U.S. into a position of military disadvantage and dangerous vulnerability. The Soviets' efforts have produced new weapons, including new generations of intercontinental ballistic missiles directly threatening our nuclear deterrent. In Europe, Soviet deployments have given the Soviet Union an overwhelming advantage over the West in this category of weapons. The freeze proposal, which is neither verifiable nor reduces weapons, is not only bad defense but bad arms control as well. The President needs the strategic modernization program if we are to have a credible chance to negotiate a good START agreement with the Soviets. The freeze would, of course, kill the modernization program and with it our chances for achieving the reductions that we all seek.[53]

START, then, could co-opt the freeze's rhetoric of peace. It became the centerpiece of the administration's Peaceful Offensive against the freeze.

In a March 30, 1982, memo, James W. Cicconi, the deputy assistant to the chief of staff, laid out this new plan to regain favorable public opinion. The administration would use the opposition's own terminology to promote their White House objectives, namely to "prevent a 'freeze' of a present Soviet advantage in nuclear weapons." Publicly, administration officials needed to avoid "calls for unilateralism" so as to "inhibit the growth of pacifist sentiment." Cicconi advised that "the way to achieve" this goal was by "co-opting the freeze movement through commitment to a freeze *at a reduced level*," or ensuring that both superpowers reduced their nuclear arsenals "before applying a freeze."[54]

This strategy to avoid unilateralism was a response to pressures not just at home but also abroad. In Great Britain, France, and West Germany, the European Nuclear Disarmament (END) group was growing in size and impact, especially with the impending delivery of US nuclear warheads to Western Europe (the so-called Euromissile Crisis examined at length in chapter 3) set for October 1983.[55] Recognizing the antinuclear movement's appeal, and hoping to put pressure on Washington, Soviet leader Leonid I. Brezhnev proposed a unilateral Soviet freeze on current levels of nuclear weapons. If Reagan rejected this offer in the face of mounting protest, he might lose public support; additionally, Brezhnev might make good on his threat to engage in an "analogous position," an ambiguous phrase that perhaps meant the installation of Soviet missiles in Cuba. It was a dangerous boast, and understandably tensions grew. The British renewed calls for Brezhnev to reconsider the deployment; in Geneva, US–Soviet talks over European

IRBMs were recessed; and back in Congress, Democrats debated the merits of a unilateral freeze after Brezhnev's remarks.[56] To avoid capitulating to calls for a freeze at home, from END in Europe, and from a Soviet leader in the Kremlin, START was a way to up the ante and promote not a freeze but an actual arms *reduction.*

The administration's strategy to promote START hinged on co-opting the freeze's rhetoric of peace—just not an actual freeze. Cicconi made this intention clear: "This is all a propaganda exercise," he assured Chief of Staff James Baker, as "the Soviets would never agree to a reduction in the present numbers of weapons they have, nor would they agree to allow the U.S. to build up their present level without further increases on their part." The public strategy, then, was to appear to appease freeze advocates while privately continuing a buildup to stand strong against Brezhnev. In executing this propaganda exercise, terminology mattered: "Unless we use the term 'freeze' in our statement we will not succeed in co-opting any significant part of the freeze movement." An actual freeze, Cicconi's reminded Baker, would be undesirable to the Soviets as it would "yield a U.S. advantage in technological advances (such as the cruise missile)." Still, there was undeniable political capital to be gained in publicly embracing the freeze: "[The] entire freeze movement rests on its simplicity (or simplistic appeal, if you will); it is thus easy to blur the distinctions between 'freeze as is' and 'reduce, then freeze' since it hinges on how one defines 'freeze.'" Therefore, "it should not matter whether or not we use the term *provided* we define it to mean what we want." Cicconi concluded that "since we control action on the issue, we still hold most of the cards. We should play them to win the propaganda battle since that is the only thing to be won or lost here."[57]

In April, the White House began its efforts to "totally neutralize" the freeze movement, but doing so would mean proceeding cautiously. In an April 16, 1982, memo to Chief of Staff Michael Deaver, Byron "Red" Cavaney, the co-deputy assistant to the president for public liaison, warned against a frontal attack on the nuclear freeze. "It may be best not to deride those who hold the freeze idea so closely," Cavaney argued, "since their beliefs may be strongly rooted in the morals of the argument." Instead, the White House should "counter the public momentum" and create a "Preparedness Working Group" to combat pro-freeze propaganda such as *The Fate of the Earth,* which promised to turn the nuclear freeze into the "the catalyst for a number of summertime demonstrations."[58]

Others shared Cavaney's concerns. On April 22, 1982, William Clark (assistant to the president for security affairs) wrote an "urgent" memo to the influential "troika" of Reagan's top first-term advisers—Chief of Staff Baker, Deputy Chief of Staff Michael Deaver, and Councilor to the President Edwin Meese III—warning that Ground Zero and a host of other antinuclear groups were pushing for "policy proposals that would be detrimental to the United States." Because "the next phase for the movement could be toward promotion of policy solutions," the White House needed to take action: "Our effort should be directed toward convincing Americans whose anxieties are heightened by this movement that *our* policy solutions best meet their desire that the United States do something to lessen the prospect of a nuclear holocaust. The time for us to do something is now, and I agree with [Assistant to the President for Communications] David Gergen that the communications effort must be pulled together by the NSC and the White House."[59]

To Clark, it was important to avoid arguing against the antinuclear movement, and especially antinuclear cultural activists like Molander: "In no way do I wish to foster a 'we/they' syndrome, wherein we become antagonists with Roger Molander of Ground Zero." Clark had to admit that Molander's approach of demystifying the nuclear threat for a wide readership worked: "[The] broad public is being awakened to the problems specialists in and out of government have dealt with for years," and for this reason "they are scared to death at the prospect of nuclear war." To co-opt the appeal of these antinuclear paperbacks, the administration should, "as Dave Gergen says . . . emphasize the President's role as a peacemaker . . . [and] focus on concrete policy and new initiatives; otherwise, our 'peace offensive' will be met with cynicism, both at home and abroad."[60]

Its rationale laid out, the implementation of the Peaceful Offensive rested on three major elements. First, "immediate efforts to enhance communication of the President's philosophy on arms control," which included radio talks "perfectly timed to present the President's views at the beginning of Ground Zero week," as well as numerous network television opportunities for administration officials, and publication of select Senate testimonies. The problem was that *Nuclear War* had provided activists across the country with common questions for the administration; now, Clark wanted to provide common answers to all top-ranking officials. Reagan, then, would not act alone in these efforts. Clark stressed that "[we should be] passing the word to our own people and briefing outside organizations and individuals on a priority basis . . . The themes must be kept basic . . . each senior official should know how to handle the issue when it comes up. More importantly, we urgently need a small, but readily available, stable of articulate people who can address the issue and guide the public." Such spokesmen should be available for "public speeches, television appearances, editorial board conferences, media interviews, and group meetings."[61]

Element number two: manage the public relations of dealing with activist groups such as Ground Zero. "Communications with the activists" should be selectively publicized. "The fact that activists have our attention should be kept secret," reminded Clark. "We want to demonstrate that we, too, are activists—seeking resolution to the same concerns." The administration needed to "make it known without fanfare that we are doing so, rather than have the media leap on the inevitable leak to portray us as secretive and defensive." In other cases, the White House would meet with activists like "Molander . . . to show the public that we are paying attention . . . to the national message of concern, and that we have the best program to deal with those concerns." [62] Doing so could reassure the public but also refocus activist energies away from public demonstrations and toward private engagement with the White House.

That led to element number three: to stress time and again, in the press and mass media, the boldness of the START initiative. "The President should restate his policy [START] as a major, but not central, part of his overall foreign policy speech, foreshadowing a new initiative in connection with START. Then, in line with Dave Gergen's suggestion, he should go on prime time to present his arms control proposals and propose a date for START . . . The television talk and our associated efforts could be the key to gaining public support from June to November. The talk should be accompanied by an all-out communications and policy coordination effort." Clark believed that this propaganda campaign was vital as the antinuclear movement had become "the most important national security opportunity and challenge of this Administration."[63]

To execute their Peaceful Offensive, Clark advised that the president conduct a "series of 'Quiet [White House] Evenings' [with] thoughtful leaders of the peace movement" to discuss nuclear issues. If so, Reagan should "utilize every opportunity to have visuals which show [him] to be the concerned, caring individual he is" and whenever possible reaffirm his peaceful stance. The administration might also publicly consult with a bipartisan figure "supportive of administration philosophy," such as Henry Kissinger, while a centralized speakers bureau could keep busy "tracking . . . public forums and media opportunities" and provide a "speaker kit to include talking points, speech inserts, speeches, graphics and handouts," along with a "mailing list for appropriate materials" and "briefings for speakers."[64]

That memo was sent April 22. Four days later, one day after Ground Zero Week concluded, Clark delivered his proposed speaker kits and talking points. In a confidential memo to President Reagan, Secretary of State Alexander Haig, Defense Secretary Caspar Weinberger, NSC Senior Defense Program Director Robert E. Linhard, and David Gergen, Clark coordinated prolonged efforts to slow the "nuclear freeze movement and the accelerating growth of anti-nuclear sentiment in this country." He stressed that "the dimensions of the nuclear freeze movement, Ground Zero Week, the Administration's difficulties over the defense budget" and other issues "require us to address the public affairs issues connected with defense and arms control in the most comprehensive fashion possible, and at the highest level." Highlighting the importance of this task, advisers met in the Situation Room on Wednesday, April 28, to prepare drafts for NSC review. Those drafts proposed the creation of public affairs "Fact Sheets and Q's and A's"; an updated inventory of "Existing Government Publications which compliment Q&A material"; another inventory of "White House Agency Resources" and sympathetic "Private Sector Resources," along with a "Legislative calendar of relevant hearings"; and "Outlines of Press Strategy on the above" alongside the "development of [an] International Information Strategy."[65] Clark even delineated the specific questions each department should answer, such as: "What is our present nuclear strategy? What does our strategy say about deterrence, war, winning, etc.?" and "What would be the impact on arms control of a reduced reliance on nuclear deterrence/weapons?" In other words, Clark didn't want any ambiguity; all administration officials needed to be prepped and ready to answer common questions with common answers.

Of special importance was the role that antinuclear paperbacks played in promoting the freeze; so, the administration should consider their own publication to counteract the criticisms found in *The Fate of the Earth, Nuclear War,* and *Freeze!* "We should be looking into the possibility of taking publications, such as *A Chronology of United States Arms Reduction Initiatives, 1946–1982* and changing it slightly to make it Congressionally acceptable for U.S. distribution. Publications such as these could probably be sent out under State auspices."[66] In 1982 the United States International Communication Agency (USICA) published *In Search of Peace: American Initiatives, 1946–1982,* a seventeen-page paperback and the beginning of a public backtrack away from the early administration hardline rhetoric. *In Search of Peace* promoted efforts not to win but to limit the arms race, and reaffirmed Reagan's refusal to consider any unilateral freeze. Citing superior Soviet strategic numbers, Reagan had recently delivered a similar message to the Canadian Parliament: "I believe we must go beyond a freeze to have reductions. A freeze under current circumstances would be a dangerously unstable and unequal strategic balance, and remove any incentive for the Soviets to reduce their arsenal."[67]

Its rhetoric in place, now the White House created a special "Nuclear Arms Control Information Policy Group" that could sustain pro-administration propaganda well into the November midterm elections. Co-chaired by Robert C. "Bud" McFarlane, deputy assistant to the president for the NSC, and William Clark, the committee's goal was to contain the influence of groups like Ground Zero, and that meant reframing the narrative to splinter freeze support. Noting that "much of the support for an immediate nuclear freeze is 'soft,'" McFarlane and Clark devised a divide-and-conquer strategy that identified different gradients of support for the freeze: "About two-fifths of the public changes its opinion from initially favoring the idea of a nuclear freeze to opposing a freeze proposal that would be unilateral," so the administration should play up fears that any freeze might "leave the U.S. even 'somewhat' behind the USSR in nuclear military strength, or be unverifiable." Fortunately for the White House, this fact "causes a near-reversal of opinion from a roughly 70-to-20 percent majority supporting the freeze idea to about a 25-to-65 percent majority opposing a freeze that is flawed in one of the above ways."[68]

There were also demographic differences at play. "One-fifth of the public is inclined to favor any nuclear freeze agreement [while] one-fifth opposes any freeze agreement," so efforts should be focused on the middle 60 percent of Americans. McFarlane and Clark agreed on whose minds they needed to change. Demographically, the "population groups most in favor of an immediate freeze are females, adults 18–29, Blacks, liberals and Democrats," while the "groups having the lowest majorities favoring a freeze are males, Southerners, conservatives, and Republicans." To change these minds, the administration should play up Americans' widespread "distrust of Soviet adherence to" a freeze resolution. Fortunately, earlier campaign rhetoric stuck, as the current public "perception of Soviet superiority in nuclear forces" combined with their "distrust of Soviet intentions [should] serve to diminish support for an immediate nuclear freeze." Finally, of special importance, authors like Schell and Molander needed to be stopped; their paperbacks had so successfully demystified strategic arguments that the White House needed to reaffirm the complexities of the atomic age, because "the general public is more inclined to believe that the nuclear freeze issue . . . is 'too complicated for the public.'" Put simply, they needed to re-complicate debates over nuclear war.[69]

All told, the administration's "Proposed National Media Strategy for Arms Control Policy" was considerable, and its ultimate goal was to stop freeze referenda from succeeding at the midterm election polls. The first vital date was "immediately after Labor Day" when Euromissile negotiators would "be available in Washington," an event likely to make national headlines. For the administration it was an "opportunity to emphasize—through joint interviews—the extent of arms reduction efforts. Not only are we negotiating reductions in strategic weapons, but in intermediate weapons and conventional forces, a comprehensive approach generally unknown to the public." As November approached, the administration had already "prepared to respond rapidly to media requests and have formulated well in advance the position we wish to take regarding the outcome." They would share this position in major news outlets including the *New York Times, Wall Street Journal, Newsweek, Washington Post,* and *US News,* and on television shows such as *Meet the Press, Good Morning America, CBS Morning News, Nightline,* and the *MacNeil/Lehrer NewsHour;* in these media, pro-administration points were provided by the conservative columnist William F. Buckley Jr., Vice President George H. W. Bush, Secretary of State Shultz, and Defense Secretary Weinberger. At every opportunity, these figures would promote the administration's new arms control policies, which, they argued, were more effective than a nuclear freeze.[70]

Then came November 2. Thanks to help from promotional and organizational tools such as *Nuclear War* and *Freeze!,* activists had put freeze referendums on the ballots in nine states, although two in particular stood out: Wisconsin, long a progressive-leaning state that had assumed a pragmatic stance on the freeze, and California, Reagan's home state, meaning that a successful freeze resolution could be seen as an indictment of the president himself. Both Wisconsin and California were essential to the Peaceful Offensive, and both states were visited by high-ranking administration officials who delivered speeches and campaigned against the freeze. At first glance, the Reagan administration seems to have lost the battle—freeze propositions passed in eight of the nine states. However, state-level freeze legislation became bogged down with quibbling over bilateral vs. unilateral disarmament; ultimately, such disagreements meant that nuclear freeze campaigners found it difficult to enact meaningful policy changes. When a freeze resolution finally reached the Senate in late 1983, it failed to meet ratification. By promoting the administration's stance and re-complicating the issue of the freeze, the Peaceful Offensive had succeeded.

The popularity of early 1980s antinuclear paperbacks so successfully fueled the freeze campaign that the White House had to respond. By the November 1982 elections, however, freeze resolutions that once looked promising were showing signs of weakness. It wasn't just the natural slowing of momentum or enthusiasm of freeze advocates, or any psychic numbing, that led to these failures; instead, it was the Reagan administration's concerted efforts, from March to November 1982, that steered public discourse away from the freeze and toward peaceful-sounding alternatives, especially START. The Peaceful Offensive did not signal any real shift in the Reagan administration's pursuit of nuclear superiority or continuation with the arms race; but it did successfully, as Cicconi had hoped, co-opt the freeze movement's rhetoric. By framing START as a morally superior step toward disarmament, the administration ensured that those not yet committed to the freeze campaign were not swayed.

If sales are any indicator, the administration's Peaceful Offensive media campaign did lower demand for antinuclear paperbacks. By November 1982, these books were no longer flying off the shelves as they had in March; according to one book buyer for the Minneapolis-based B. Dalton Booksellers, "We probably bought about 40 different books on the subject, but we bought modest numbers of all but two or three, and that's how they've been selling—modestly." Dalton stores nationwide reported similar sales, and chain stores had even less success than college bookstores. According to a buyer for the State University of New York at Brockport bookstore, in the spring of 1982 atomic anxiety led the university to require "that for general-education courses all entering freshmen have to buy *Nuclear War: What's in It for You?*"[71] There was no such requirement for the group's 1983 follow-up mass-market paperback *What about the Russians—and Nuclear War?*

Some scholars have assessed the freeze movement's inability to enact meaningful political changes as evidence that Lifton's "psychic numbing" was real, that such serious and prolonged antinuclear activism simply could not be sustained.[72] However, that decline in zeal—evidenced by the decline of antinuclear paperback sales, a barometer of overall public interest in the freeze—was in part the result of White House efforts to promote going beyond a freeze and seek arms reductions via START. By November 1982, thanks to the efforts of Cicconi, Clark, Baker, and others, the nuclear threat seemed less pronounced. The Peaceful Offensive had worked.

The antinuclear book boom of 1982 was, however, only the opening salvo in a media war between cultural activists and the Reagan administration. These paperbacks and the grassroots protests they helped to catalyze may have failed to result in meaningful freeze resolutions, but it took considerable effort by the White House to contain their impact. After the midterm elections of November 1982, the antinuclear media war would continue. In 1983, the celebrity scientist Carl Sagan began a crusade to demonstrate the illogic of the arms race. He did so by promoting a new scientific vision of the apocalypse: nuclear winter.

2

The Nuclear Winter

Carl Sagan introduced the term "Nuclear Winter" to millions of Americans in the October 30, 1983, edition of *Parade Magazine*. The term describes a post–nuclear war scenario in which massive fires send radioactive soot and ash into the atmosphere. In the days and weeks that follow, these particulates would encircle the globe and block sunlight, leaving the world in a prolonged state of cold and darkness, destroying vegetation and rendering agriculture impossible. Such a global environmental catastrophe, Sagan argued, might occur even after a limited nuclear war.[1] Although Sagan worked with a cohort of reputable scientists and followed traditional methods of peer review, presenting these findings in a national newspaper inset—*Parade* was distributed inside of *USA Today*—was unorthodox. This, along with Sagan's other publicity tactics, reveals a clear goal: to go beyond a scientific readership and argue for disarmament directly to a critical mass of the American public. Sagan believed that science might sway millions of Americans to reject Reagan's arms buildup; if only they knew the catastrophic risks of even a limited nuclear war, which the Reagan administration had boasted it could wage and win, the American public might engage in activism and end the arms race.

Because it combined science with political activism, nuclear winter remains a curious theory. This story has been examined in two Sagan biographies, although both assess Sagan's activism as little more than a well-intentioned misstep in an otherwise outstanding career.[2] More recently, the historian Paul Rubinson has reaffirmed the importance of Sagan's theory in renewing Cold War scientific activism. Like Paul Boyer in *By the Bomb's Early Light*, which traced scientists' efforts in the late 1940s to control atomic energy and weaponry, Rubinson shows that in the 1980s the concept of nuclear winter allowed scientists to reengage in politics and promote an arms-control agenda in not just the United States but also the Soviet Union.[3] Lawrence Badash's *A Nuclear Winter's Tale* similarly views Sagan's promotion of the theory as "an exemplar of twentieth-century interaction between science and society," although ultimately these efforts were sabotaged by "Big Science," or the growing bureaucratic nature of peer review and government involvement in scientific inquiry.[4]

Others draw parallels with the efforts of Big Tobacco, which since the 1940s pitted private industries against scientific critics. In *The Cigarette Century,* Allan Brandt explains, "By making science fair game in the battle of public relations, the tobacco industry set a destructive precedent that would affect future debate on subjects ranging from global warming to intelligent design." In other words, "the tobacco industry's PR campaign permanently changed both science and public culture."[5] In their 2009 book *Merchants of Doubt,* Naomi Oreskes and Erik M. Conway see connections between the nuclear winter controversy and later debates over global climate change. Finally, Wilfried Mausbach has argued that nuclear winter was a product of an emerging global ecological consciousness, setting it apart from previous local or regional environmental causes. Clearly, the nuclear winter story is one with many facets, encompassing Cold War politics, science, and environmentalism.[6]

While these assessments of the nuclear winter hypothesis uncover the blurring lines between politics and science in the 1980s, they tend to overlook how effective Sagan was in promoting disarmament to the public and world political leaders. In promoting this idea in popular publications, Sagan made a devil's bargain—one that traded credibility for publicity; however, Sagan's pleas for a global reduction of the nuclear stockpile gained traction abroad and threatened America's Cold War alliances. In response, the NSC crafted a strategy to discredit Sagan, handpicking scientific "experts" to attack his media campaign as clear evidence of bad science. From October 1983 until late 1985, Sagan's efforts to promote the theory of nuclear winter were not ineffectual, but they were thwarted by an administration that accepted the validity of a nuclear winter scenario while it simultaneously co-opted Sagan's theory to endorse their need for a strong deterrent.

Rather than debate the validity of nuclear winter as a scientific hypothesis—which numerous scientists writing in the early 1980s certainly did—in this chapter I examine the efforts to market and promote a scientific theory that endorsed disarmament.[7] These efforts were so singular that any such discussion has to begin with Carl Sagan himself. He was the indispensable figure—the only scientific activist of the era who could combine science, Cold War culture, global environmentalism, and disarmament politics into a new, marketable antinuclear concept for the 1980s. A brief examination of his life reveals the numerous influences that made this possible.

Carl Sagan and the Creation of Nuclear Winter

Carl Edward Sagan was born in Brooklyn in 1934. From a young age he excelled academically, and like many Atomic Age teenagers, developed a love of science fiction, especially from the magazine *Astounding Science Fiction*. His biographers recount that Sagan spent "long, happy hours reading" the magazine and that his "love of *Astounding* continued well into college." Admitted to the University of Chicago in 1951, Sagan earned his MS (1956) and his PhD (1960) in astronomy and astrophysics under the supervision of the astronomer Gerard Kuiper.[8] Throughout these years, Sagan maintained his "enormous interest in science fiction," his dorm room littered with copies of the magazine.[9] These were the early years of the Cold War, and like many sci-fi publications, *Astounding* printed its fair share of nuclear war stories— some purely dystopian, but some with fairly accurate scientific details. *Astounding*'s editor at the time was John W. Campbell Jr., who had trained as a physicist at MIT and understood atomic science; in March 1944, a year before the first successful atomic test, Campbell published a story narrating the construction of an atomic bomb that was so accurate it earned him a visit from War Department security officials. Many of *Astounding*'s contributions shared Campbell's technical acumen, filled with the kind of minutia that a young scientist and sci-fi fan like Sagan could appreciate.[10]

In April 1957 *Astounding Science Fiction* published "Torch" by Christopher Anvil, a story that depicts a scenario strikingly similar to nuclear winter. After a Soviet intercontinental ballistic launch goes wrong, a "groundhog" bunker-buster missile ignites underground oil reserves, starting a fire that sends particulates into the atmosphere. Sagan would have read "Torch" while studying atmospheric science and likely appreciated Anvil's specificity, especially references to "carbon monoxide; carbon dioxide; water vapor; saturated and unsaturated gaseous hydrocarbons; the vapors of saturated and unsaturated nongaseous hydrocarbons [and] soot." Anvil's use of a bunker-buster bomb was also timely, considering America's 1950s bomb shelter craze.[11] "Torch" concludes with the superpowers setting aside ideological differences and joining forces to extinguish the gigantic fire; however, the smog belt remains in the atmosphere, blocking sunlight and lowering temperatures to one hundred degrees below zero. In the last scene, "heavily dressed delegates of the former 'Communist' and 'Capitalist' blocs" meet to commemorate the end of the first "cold war" but also to take a "solemn pledge to 'Remain united as one people under God, and to persevere in our efforts together till and even beyond the time when the *Cold War* shall end.'" This idea, that global environmental catastrophe could cut through political ideology, would be a key element of Sagan's later efforts to promote disarmament.[12]

In addition to science fiction, Sagan was also a fan of the work of the space artist Chesley Bonestell. In an era before NASA perfected space photography, Bonestell specialized in painting planets, stars, nebulae, and black holes. He was perhaps the best known planetary artist of the century, earning the title "Grand Master of astronomical artists." Later in life, Sagan purchased a considerable Bonestell collection for his Ithaca, New York, home.[13] Of these works, one stands out: an image of New York City under atomic attack. It first appeared in a 1948 *Collier's* piece by Robert S. Richardson titled "Rocket Blitz from the Moon" with the accompanying caption: "Two one-megaton-yield nuclear warheads explode over the New York metropolitan area. Dark, sooty fires are set substantial distances away." The imposition of giant mushroom clouds—an image that quickly became the iconic symbol of atomic power and destruction—over a New York City set ablaze with giant sooty fires would have made an impression on many Cold War-era readers. Decades later, Sagan would describe similar "dark, sooty fires" as a trigger for nuclear winter.[14]

Completing his PhD in 1960, Sagan started along a predictable career path for a Cold War astrophysicist. With a recommendation from his adviser, he went to work at the Armour Research Foundation at the Illinois Institute of Technology in Chicago, where one of his tasks was to model "the expansion of an exploding gas/dust cloud rarifying into the space around the Moon." He also served as a consultant for the Rand Corporation, and in 1962 completed a postdoc at UC Berkeley. It was the height of the Cold War, a year in which nuclear fears reached new levels during the October Cuban missile crisis. A year later, President Kennedy was assassinated, and his successor, Lyndon B. Johnson, escalated America's military involvement in Vietnam. Throughout the 1960s, Sagan grew increasingly disillusioned with government-funded projects, especially for weapons systems; he rejected numerous military contracts, a staple for Cold War scientists seeking funding.[15] It was a conscious choice that reflected his increasing interest in political activism and, to a lesser degree, the counterculture. As an undergraduate, Sagan canvassed for the Democratic Party, taught science seminars in Tuskegee, Alabama, during the civil rights movement, and by the mid-1960s was active in Vietnam War protests; he also started smoking marijuana. Politicized after a turbulent decade, Sagan turned to Linus Pauling, the Nobel Prize–winning chemist who in the 1950s warned Americans about the pernicious effects of radioactive fallout, as a role model: the scientist as activist.[16]

In addition to his political activities, Sagan stayed busy teaching and conducting research. By 1968, after a stint at the Smithsonian Astrophysical Observatory in Cambridge, Massachusetts, he joined the faculty of Cornell University. Now a professor of planetary studies, Sagan—like most Americans—became fascinated with the *Apollo 8* spacecraft's photographs that captured Earth from space. This "Pale Blue Dot" was featured on the cover of the January 10, 1969, issue of *Life*. Also known as the "Blue Marble" or "Spaceship Earth" photograph, it symbolized humanity's growing awareness of an interconnected planet. In his later efforts to promote the nuclear winter theory, Sagan often referred to "Spaceship Earth": "From Earth's orbit, you are struck by the tender blue arc of the horizon—the Earth's thin atmosphere seen tangentially. You can understand why there is no longer such a thing as a local environmental problem." Such global environmental language became common in the 1970s; even President Richard Nixon remarked that Americans were "growing accustomed to the view of our planet as seen from space; no matter what else divides men and nations, this perspective should unite them."[17]

All of these influences formed in Sagan the belief that science could unite people of different races, religions, and ideologies; it was a message he began to promote in his work. In 1977, Sagan earned a Pulitzer Prize for his book *The Dragons of Eden,* and he became a frequent guest on Johnny Carson's *Tonight Show,* propelling his popularity to new heights. By 1981, outgoing President Jimmy Carter asked Sagan to contribute to his farewell address, to which Sagan offered the following lines: "Nuclear weapons are an expression of one side of our human character. But there's another side. The same rocket technology that delivers nuclear warheads has also taken us peacefully into space. From this perspective, we see our Earth as it really is—a small and fragile and beautiful blue globe, the only home we have. We see no barriers of race or religion or country."[18] This was the interconnected world that Sagan longed for; he hated the arms race, the acrimony of the Cold War, and the threat of nuclear war. During Reagan's presidency, the nuclear winter hypothesis would provide Sagan an opportunity to combat all three issues under the auspices of science.

The idea of nuclear winter began to take shape in 1971 with Sagan's involvement in NASA's *Mariner* explorations, which captured the first images of Mars. Sagan's role was to explain these findings to journalists, who gravitated toward the young, charismatic scientist. He had a gift for explaining the complexities of space in accessible language and captured the public's imagination by proposing that Mars held more promise for life (albeit bacterial life) than any other planet in our solar system.[19] But behind all the promotional work, Sagan was doing actual science, specifically with *Mariner*'s data readings. The satellite's Infrared Interferometric Spectrometer—an instrument that records atmospheric particulate levels—indicated unusually high dust levels in the Martian atmosphere but low temperatures on its surface. Sagan made the connection: particulates were blocking sunlight and cooling the planet's surface. He wondered if such phenomena could occur on Earth.[20]

To investigate this possibility, Sagan picked a team of scientific experts: Richard Turco, a researcher at Ames National Laboratory who had already published papers on the effects nuclear weapons blasts might have on the ozone layer; James Pollack, a Sagan protégé who left Cornell for Ames; Thomas Ackerman, also at Ames, who wrote a doctoral thesis on Venus's greenhouse gasses; and Owen Brian Toon, who wrote a doctoral thesis on Earth and Martian climate change. It was a gifted team, but these scientists faced a problem: this was a hypothetical scenario, one that relied heavily on nascent computer modeling technology—not an inexpensive proposition at the time—and historical precedents, such as the 1815 volcanic eruption on the Philippine island of Tambora. The Tambora blast spread particulates into the atmosphere, blocking sunlight and lowering global temperatures; in England, Lord Byron recorded 1816 as the "year without a summer." Sagan's team initially began to ponder if aerosols, such as chlorofluorocarbons (CFCs) emitted from common household products and commercial airliners, might contribute to climate change.[21]

After this preliminary inquiry, three scientific reports emerged that shifted the team's focus from consumer products to nuclear weapons. The first, a 1975 US National Academy of Sciences report titled "The Long-Term Worldwide Effects of Multiple Nuclear Weapons Detonations," considered not just the immediate effects of global thermonuclear war (such as heat, blast, and fire) but the long-term ecological aftereffects. In 1979 a second report, the US Congressional Office of Technology Assessment publication "The Effects of Nuclear War," focused on the atmospheric consequences of atomic detonations. Third, in 1980 the physicist Luis Alvarez and a group of UC Berkeley scientists argued that some 65 million years ago, a giant meteor struck Earth, sent masses of particulates into the atmosphere, blocking sunlight and freezing vegetation. This new dinosaur "extinction theory" quickly gained scientific acceptance, spawning some two thousand related articles and books over the next ten years.[22] Sagan read these reports with great interest. Now his team would refocus to investigate the *environmental* impact of a nuclear war.[23]

As Sagan's group worked to apply Alvarez's theory to nuclear war, another team preempted their efforts. In 1982, two scientists—Paul Crutzen of the Max Planck Institute for Chemistry in Mainz, West Germany, and John Birks of the University of Colorado—coauthored an article titled "The Atmosphere after a Nuclear War: Twilight at Noon." Crutzen and Birks argued that it was not simply smoke, but also the soot and ash from fires caused by atomic blasts that could trigger catastrophic global atmospheric and environmental changes. Even more, it would not take a total nuclear war but only a limited nuclear exchange to increase global levels of UV-B radiation, triggering composition changes in the troposphere and causing stratospheric ozone depletion.[24] The same year as the Crutzen-Birks essay, the leaders of three philanthropic foundations—the Rockefeller Family Fund, the Audubon Society, and the Henry P. Kendall Foundation—funded a study of the long-term biological consequences of nuclear war. They recruited Sagan, who had access to NASA's Ames Research Center and its supercomputers, which were capable of newly emerging modeling technology. The initial simulations hinted that Crutzen and Birks were right: even a limited nuclear war could have global environmental consequences. The implication of such findings meant that even nations left untouched in a nuclear war would later perish from its aftereffects.[25]

By 1983, all the elements were there. Sagan had brought together a cohort of scientists who, utilizing their access to Ames supercomputers, were taking the findings of Alvarez et. al. and Crutzen-Birks and applying them to an escalating arms race. Not all of Sagan's team had strong political opinions, nor did they all seek to engage in activism. But for Sagan, the issue of arms reductions was too pressing, especially after President Reagan promised to put weapons in space (with SDI, the focus of chapter 4). What he needed was a concerted, coordinated media campaign, and that meant gaining needed access to mass media outlets. Luckily, by 1983, Sagan was a well-recognized public figure. His book *Cosmos* and its accompanying 1982 PBS series had become the most read, and most watched, scientific works of their day, and Sagan had become a frequent contributor to the popular Sunday newspaper inset *Parade Magazine,* which reached an estimated eighty million readers each week. In short, in the early 1980s, Sagan was a trusted and instantly recognizable figure in American life, and he had the capability to reach millions. Now, Sagan was going to do what he did best: take the complexities of a scientific idea and repackage it for a popular audience.[26]

Marketing Nuclear Winter

It might seem cynical to discuss the "marketing" of a scientific hypothesis, but the term should not imply that Sagan was peddling bad science. Rather, he sought to present complex science to the lay public. "Nuclear winter" itself was a marketable phrase, albeit one born of political necessity. It wasn't Sagan's, but the creation of his collaborator Richard Turco, who in 1983 completed a final draft of the group's findings, "The Environmental Consequences of Nuclear War," which he was about to submit for peer review. Because the report "had to go through a vetting process at NASA," Turco worried that any mention of nuclear war would raise red flags for "a very conservative government." He was right; NASA refused to let the phrase "nuclear war" be included in report's original title. So, Turco improvised: "At the last minute I had to come up with a new title." Imagining the cold, dark, and radioactive the state of the Earth's atmosphere after a nuclear war, he coined "nuclear winter."[27]

Turco's phrase provided a new imaginative landscape of a post-apocalyptic world. Cold War atomic culture had long offered images of the apocalypse. In films, literature, and comic books, nuclear apocalypse conveyed death through atomic blast, heat, and the invisible poison of radiation.[28] "Nuclear winter" offered a new image, in which humanity is destroyed not by heat or blast but by extreme cold and darkness. It seemed an unlikely pairing, and in joining "nuclear" with "winter" Turco had created a "catachresis," or "the use of a word in some new sense in order to remedy a gap in the vocabulary; the putting of new senses into old words."[29] Sagan immediately recognized the power of Turco's language—it was certainly shorter, and catchier, than the original report's title; as one Sagan biographer assessed, nuclear winter "did a lot to sell a highly complex idea."[30]

Alongside Turco's new atomic term, Sagan crafted a marketable acronym for his scientific cohort. Arranging the authors' surnames in the following order—Turco, Toon, Ackerman, Pollack, and Sagan—spelled TTAPS. Pronounced "taps," it referenced the military bugle call played at lights-out, as well as at funerals, and provided Sagan with yet another useful cultural reference in a media campaign laden with cold and dark imagery. The TTAPS team predicted that using a baseline scenario of a 5,000 megaton exchange—then roughly one-third of the superpower arsenal—massive fires would send plumes of thick, sooty smoke into the atmosphere, dropping global temperature by 25 degrees Celsius, sending Earth into a deepfreeze that could last for weeks with daytime light levels reduced by 95 percent. Considering these "lights out" predications, TTAPS was a fitting acronym.[31]

Sagan's selection of high-notoriety collaborators was another important part of his efforts to market nuclear winter. Recognizing that the interdisciplinary nature of this study would require not just atmospheric scientists but also biologists, Sagan asked Stanford's Paul Ehrlich to participate. It was an auspicious choice. Ehrlich was already a widely recognized public figure from his 1968 best seller *The Population Bomb,* a book that predicted global catastrophe from a human reproduction cycle spinning out of control. In the 1970s, Ehrlich became the key figure in the controversial group he helped establish, Zero Population Growth, which linked ecological salvation and biological preservation with a global reproductive restraint—a controversial proposition, both then and today.[32] Like Sagan, in the 1980s Ehrlich shifted focus to curbing the arms race, as his 1982 article promoting disarmament in the *Bulletin of Atomic Scientists* made clear.[33] Therefore, the selection of Ehrlich added even more media notoriety to the usually innocuous process of peer review; science writers speculated that Sagan's selection of Ehrlich helped to get nuclear winter "on page one" in American media.[34]

With the pieces in place, Sagan now conceived a nuclear winter media blitz. It began with an informal review held in Cambridge in April 1983; afterward, Sagan submitted TTAPS's frightening predictions to a reputable journal, *Science,* which slated the article for its December 1983 issue alongside an Ehrlich-supervised report on the biological consequences of nuclear war. This would be a relatively quick turnaround for peer review, raising suspicions of a hasty submission; but timing was important, and Sagan planned on going public with these findings as soon as possible.[35] The venue: a well-publicized conference set to take place over two days (October 30–31) in Washington, DC. This public peer-review session would coincide with a summary of the TTAPS findings Sagan submitted for the Halloween edition of *Parade Magazine*. It was a move that garnered publicity, but also criticism; as the MIT political scientist George Rathjens put it, "in the scientific community you don't publish first results in *Parade* magazine."[36]

To maximize publicity for the Halloween events, Sagan contacted Porter Novelli, a public relations firm with a successful history of working with government agencies, NGOs, and nonprofits. According to the firm's chairman, Jack Porter, Sagan began planning this media blitz almost immediately after the Cambridge conference. "We felt from the beginning that we had an important story," he recalled. "If we concentrated our efforts on the 25 or 30 major media and we defined those as the network news shows, the morning shows, some specific discussion shows like *Donohue* and *Nightline*," then nuclear winter could reach a national audience. Sagan also pursued other "high-visibility media" including "metropolitan newspapers, the wire services [and] of course, news magazines." By enlisting Porter Novelli, Sagan made clear his desire not just to persuade a small cadre of scientific experts, but millions of Americans.[37]

Funding for the media blitz came largely from a sympathetic donor, Robert Allen of the Kendall Foundation. According to Jack Porter, the initial publicity budget was roughly $40,000, but "as we got into it, we were called upon to do a lot of other things" with final costs somewhere "in the $100,000 range."[38] How did this amount compare with other notable scientific endeavors? NASA routinely spent much more on publicity than what Sagan spent on promoting the nuclear winter theory but received comparatively little criticism. Even by the late 1990s, NASA still routinely allotted $100,000 to publicize launches.[39] In short, Porter Novelli's funding for a private scientific media campaign was considerable, but not excessive. These funds were allocated to three priorities: promoting the October 30, 1983, Washington, DC, conference; paying artists and composers to create nuclear winter animations, paintings, and multimedia scores; and establishing a one-time, high-tech satellite linkup with Soviet scientists, the so-called Moscow Link, an expensive proposition in the pre-internet years. Turco fondly remembers the extent of Sagan's efforts: "This whole event of 'the cold and the dark' [i.e., the conference] was designed to roll out this whole theory. It was a remarkable thing."[40]

For the conference, and for his subsequent public talks, Sagan oversaw the creation of multimedia aids that could transform TTAPS's sterile science into captivating imagery. Porter Novelli was up to the task; it had already designed the food pyramid diagram ubiquitous in 1980s high school health classes. Sagan understood the power of images to captivate minds; just as Chelsey Bonestell's work had affected him decades ago, Sagan's series *Cosmos* used impressive graphics to drive home complex science. To create such cold and dark artistry, Porter Novelli commissioned a nearby art firm, Wood Ronsaville Harlin. Pamela Ronsaville remembers that while her firm "had done other jobs for Porter Novelli," the group had never worked on any project with such serious overtones. The landscape artist Rob Wood recalls that when Porter Novelli called in 1983, he had "never really [done] anything that involved before. When they told me what I had to do [with nuclear winter], I knew it was going to be a big deal." Ehrlich was Wood's primary contact, and the Stanford biologist was "pretty specific in what he wanted. [He] would give us written descriptions [such as] show what it would be like if the crops were dying; show a granary in which people steal food; people salvaging [*sic*] for food, and then the cold, the extreme cold."[41] In addition to his guidance, both Wood and Ronsaville did extensive research, studying photographs of real natural disasters. Wood's goal was "make the earth after a nuclear winter to really strike home . . . about how horrible [nuclear winter] could be." Ronsaville presented Wood's images in Washington for Sagan and Ehrlich. "I gave a sales pitch," she recalls. "There were about twenty or thirty men sitting around a conference table. Sagan was there." After seeing the submissions, Sagan handpicked Wood's work for the upcoming Halloween conference slideshow presentation, and these images would also appear in the first book on nuclear winter, *The Cold and the Dark*.[42]

Next, Sagan wanted artistic depictions of a nuclear winter from space. He called the illustrator Jon Lomberg, a longtime friend who had first worked with Sagan on his 1972 book *The Cosmic Connection* and who later became chief artist on *Cosmos*. Assessing his nuclear winter work some thirty years later, Lomberg believes that his images "played at least some role in stimulating the widespread discussion and debate that followed," in that they allowed "non-scientists [to] visualize the mechanism that would cause a nuclear winter." In designing these images, Sagan worked as a collaborator. "I did it all with Carl," remembers Lomberg. "He would explain to me the science, the meaning, and the audience . . . in this case that was a non-technical audience." NASA space photography—such as the 1968 "Pale Blue Dot" image—also influenced Lomberg's work: "The images of Earth and its beauty and complexity had become iconic worldwide. The look of the Earth was definitely inspired by the real Earth." These images were featured on the cover of *Parade*

Magazine, in Ehrlich's article for *Co-Evolution Quarterly,* and in a short slide show Sagan used in university speaking engagements and in meetings with world leaders. If Sagan's decision to use alarming images in *Parade Magazine* aimed to jolt readers, it had the desired effect. *Parade* was the second-most widely read weekly periodical in the United States, and its editors received more than fifty thousand letters from concerned Americans.[43]

Sagan also incorporated these artworks into a five-minute short film, *The Global Environmental Consequences of Nuclear War.* Lomberg acted as producer, the composer Bob Derkach provided the soundtrack, and Sagan's wife, Ann Druyan, helped with graphic design. The stated goal of this presentation wasn't to convey cold scientific data, but to elicit an emotional response. By today's standards, these were low-tech affairs. Lomberg remembers that this 1983 presentation consisted of a "multi-image show . . . which is a technique that has gone the way of the slide rule. You have banks of slide projectors and it is all programmed for the slides . . . they come in a certain order with a soundtrack." But film versions of the show exist, capturing Derkach's dreary synth-soundtrack and Sagan's overdubbed narration:

> Life on earth is intimately connected with the environment, and fundamentally dependent on it. Animals depend on plants; plants depend on sunlight and weather; sunlight and weather are in turn determined by the nature and behavior of the atmosphere. These delicate relationships would be torn, perhaps irreparably, by the effects of a nuclear war. Even a small nuclear war would produce huge plumes of thick, sooty smoke; burning plastics and other synthetics would produce a wide variety of toxic gasses. The fires would burn for weeks. Thousands of smoke plumes carried downwind and merging with one another would blanket northern mid-latitudes within days . . . disturbing the climate on a global scale. For months there would be a dark, deadly nuclear winter.[44]

This evocative, dark imagery was a far cry from the sterile language found in scientific journals, such as *Science* and *Nature;* clearly, Sagan was aiming to connect with a mass audience. Druyan remembers "conversations Carl and I had, about making the consequences real to the people who lived in all those cities. It required showing what would really happen. If you really want to reach people, you've got to move them emotionally, as well as intellectually. If you don't raise goose bumps, you're not doing your job. If you say a one-degree temperature drop globally, people are going to say 'big deal,' so we had to make it so that the real consequences were visualized." To drive home those consequences, the film features frigid, desolate landscapes, a cloud-shrouded earth, and pictures of dead deer and frozen fruit. These were unsettling visuals, aimed at alarming average citizens about the threat of nuclear winter. With his propaganda pieces in place, Sagan embarked on the nuclear winter "media blitz."[45]

Nuclear Winter Media Blitz Under Way

As Halloween approached, Porter Novelli's New York office was "licking its chops . . . to set up interviews" with major news sources. Sagan planned interviews with the *New York Times* and *Newsweek* and wrote or co-wrote articles for *Science* and *Foreign Policy*. Porter Novelli was also busy, sending out press releases in mid-September 1983 to promote an extensive campaign scheduled for late October.[46] On October 30, 1983, *Parade* published Sagan's nuclear winter article, introducing for the first time this new vision of the nuclear apocalypse to the general public. Sagan may have anticipated backlash from the scientific community for this choice, but the payoff was too alluring to pass up: *Parade* guaranteed a readership of 80 million.[47]

Sagan had hoped that the nuclear winter conference would garner at least a two-day headline story, but fate intervened. In the fall of 1983 on the small Caribbean island of Grenada, Cuban-funded Marxists executed Prime Minister Maurice Bishop. Concerned for the eight hundred American medical students on the island and still reeling from a devastating terrorist attack on the marine barracks in Beirut, Lebanon, Reagan sent a seven-thousand-man force to rescue the students and expel the communists. That was October 25, less than a week before Sagan's Halloween conference, and Grenada dominated newspaper headlines, as did footage of grateful med students returning to America.[48] The invasion effectively denied the nuclear winter conference front-page newspaper headlines and prompted *Time* to postpone its coverage of the Halloween conference by a week. Jack Porter recalled the futility of requesting headline coverage at news outlets, with one reporter simply responding: "You're talking about a scientific conference? I got dead Marines here!"[49]

Despite these setbacks, on Monday, October 31, Sagan and Ehrlich appeared on ABC's *Evening News* for a two-minute piece describing their findings, with a special edition of *Nightline* examining the nuclear winter hypothesis set for the next night. In it, host Ted Koppel joined Sagan and Ehrlich to film the program from the Washington conference. The on-location production had its advantages. It allowed the Soviet scientist Sergei

Kapista to appear on American network news via the Moscow–Washington hotline. Kapista was the Soviet equivalent of Sagan, a Russian science communicator and television personality. He was also the son of Pyotr Kapista, a nuclear scientist and Nobel Laureate who once refused Stalin's request to create a copy of the American-designed atomic bomb. Kapista's participation through the Moscow Link added an element of technological spectacle to the televised event and emphasized superpower solidarity. Jack Porter remarked that Kapista and MOLINK were central to this "international strategy [that] targeted the key international press." The message was clear: science could transcend Cold War ideology.[50]

Such symbols of superpower coexistence might be persuasive; however, they were not cheap. Porter estimated that the satellite link cost an "equivalent amount" as the initial marketing funds—in other words, an additional $40,000—but for Sagan it was money well spent. A planetary scientist, Sagan viewed the world not as battleground for geopolitics, but an interconnected ecosystem. The Moscow Link was an important symbol of better superpower relations. Druyan remembers MOLINK as "part of this idea . . . ways in which we could break down the idea of enemy camps and create an atmosphere—kind of a planetary perspective—that we're all in this together." This show of Cold War comity was rare in the early eighties; consider that *Time* magazine's "Men of the Year" cover for 1983 featured Soviet President Yuri Andropov and Ronald Reagan . . . standing back to back. In a year in which superpower negotiations seemed to have broken down completely, Sagan's hope that science could bridge ideology was timely.[51]

Nightline provided Sagan with his first chance to argue with two skeptics of the nuclear winter theory: Assistant Secretary of State Richard Burt and the nuclear scientist Edward Teller. Sagan began the exchange by arguing that the specter of nuclear winter might persuade world leaders to reduce their global nuclear stockpiles. Kapitsa agreed, and stressed that Soviet scientists also believed that nuclear winter was a valid theory, while Ehrlich emphasized that nuclear war would lead to global ecological catastrophe. When Koppel queried Teller for a response, the longtime nuclear proponent stressed that his institution (the Lawrence Livermore National Laboratory) had performed similar studies as TTAPS but reached less catastrophic results. Instead of disarming to prevent a nuclear winter, Teller and Burt endorsed Reagan's SDI program. In this way, the *Nightline* episode set the stage for future nuclear winter debates that pitted Sagan against SDI proponents. For this reason, Sagan was getting the White House's attention. Internal memoranda reveal that numerous members of the Reagan administration—including Robert McFarlane, Ronald Lehman, and John Poindexter—received portions of the show's transcripts. They were already building a strategy to combat the possible negative effects of ABC's antinuclear drama *The Day After* as well as Sagan's new theory and its possible effect on public opinion.[52]

Koppel again invited Sagan for the roundtable discussion that immediately followed the November 20, 1983, airing of ABC's *The Day After*. By that point, the two had become friends, with Sagan now the newsman's "go-to guy" for all scientific issues; they frequently dined together and discussed politics.[53] *The Day After* had an estimated viewership of 100 million and ABC predicted that *Viewpoint* would keep an estimated two-thirds of that audience, or roughly 60 million viewers. Sagan had an opportunity to explain the TTAPS findings to a record-setting television audience, and he wasn't going to pass it up. When Koppel asked if there were any "merit in this movie or is the movie simply an exercise in emotionalism which might cause despair," Sagan responded by pivoting to an explanation of nuclear winter:

> I think that in this country we've been sleepwalking during the last thirty-eight years and passed this problem without really coming to grips with how dire and compelling it is, and I think that ABC should be congratulated for spurring what I hope will be a yearlong debate on this issue, but it's my unhappy duty to point out that the reality is much worse than what has been portrayed in this movie and this new emerging reality has significant policy implications. The nuclear winter that will follow even a small nuclear war . . . especially if cities are targeted as they almost certainly would be, involves a pall of dust and smoke which would reduce the temperatures not just in the northern mid-latitudes but pretty much globally, to sub-freezing temperatures for months. In addition, it's dark, the radiation from radioactivity is much more than we've been told before, agriculture would be wiped out, and it's very clear that beyond the one or two billion people who'd be killed directly in a major nuclear war—five, seven thousand megatons, something like that—the overall consequences would be much more dire, and the biologists who've been studying this think that there is a real possibility of the extinction of the human species from such a war.[54]

When Sagan stressed that the potential for a nuclear winter might have policy implications, the conservative commentator William F. Buckley interjected: "I think that what [Sagan] said is very good news. If the Soviet Union knows that any first strike will mean the extinction of the Soviet Union then there won't be a first strike." Sagan replied, "I agree with that. I'm amazed to find myself agreeing with Mr. Buckley but that is absolutely right." Because a nuclear winter could occur with the detonation of only 100 megatons, "the only prudent policy is to get well below that threshold so that no concatenation of computer failure and communications malfunction and madness in high office could kill everybody on the planet." If not, argued Sagan, you have a "circumstance in which you can end the human endeavor." Disarmament was the only solution, so for Sagan, Reagan's arms buildup meant that America was "going in the wrong direction."[55]

After his appearance on *Viewpoint,* Sagan embarked on a university speaking tour that featured a nuclear winter multimedia presentation. He also courted celebrity endorsements, which he got after presenting *The Global Environmental Consequences of Nuclear War* to "a gathering of Hollywood liberals" at the home of actress Blythe Danner and producer Bruce Paltrow— Jon Lomberg even recalls that a young Gwyneth Paltrow helped him set up the projector. The Hollywood approach paid dividends, as Sagan's nuclear winter media presentation won over numerous celebrities. Paul Newman "wanted to nominate [the film] for a special Oscar." The film also earned Lomberg some acclaim; in 1985 it received First Prize at the Vermont World Peace Film Festival.[56]

Celebrity endorsements in tow, Sagan went after broad public support, appearing on the popular Sunday CBS news show *Face the Nation.* Joined by Senator William Proxmire (D-WI), former secretary of defense James R. Schlesinger, and George Carrier, a member of the National Academy of Science, Sagan again warned of the nuclear winter threat. That week's moderator, Fred Graham (substituting for the show's regular host, Leslie Stahl) asked whether or not US nuclear policy should "be changed in light of the prospects of a lethal nuclear winter." Sagan agreed that it should, and specifically that the United States should begin to seek arms reductions. Senator Proxmire concurred: "The changes for policy seem to be to me crystal clear, and . . . we should emphasize arms control . . . to prevent nuclear war." This *Face the Nation* appearance did more than publicize the TTAPS findings; it showed that Sagan was reaching congressional leaders.[57]

Sagan's frenzied activism continued by presenting *The Global Environmental Consequences of Nuclear War* to numerous political and military leaders across the globe, including screenings at the "Canadian Parliament . . . the Supreme Soviet in Moscow . . . West Point, Annapolis, and Colorado Springs." Many were receptive to Sagan, even Pope John Paul II. Sagan's greatest success, however, came after a 1984 visit to New Zealand, where his presentation helped to convince Prime Minister David Lange to ban all nuclear-powered ships from his country's ports. The ban had deeper roots than fears of a nuclear winter—Australia and New Zealand had long histories of antinuclear activism—but Sagan's presentation helped to convince Lange that any superpower nuclear exchange would doom his country, even if it was not attacked directly. The prime minister "explicitly showed . . . the [film's] images" to members of Parliament "as part of his rationale for denying U.S. warships carrying nukes permission to harbor in his country."[58] Then, on September 24, 1984, Lange made clear his belief in the nuclear winter hypothesis to the United Nations General Assembly: "Within the last year . . . reputable scientists from east and west have told us that the global, climatic and long-term biological consequences of a nuclear war would be much more severe than had been previously thought. What is more, that would be the case if even a relatively small part of the existing nuclear arsenals were used. The scientists have also told us that nuclear war in the north may generate a nuclear winter in the south. They have gone further and advised us that there is a possibility of the self-inflicted extinction of the human species." Lange concluded by saying that not just New Zealand but Australia and eleven other South Pacific countries would join a "nuclear free zone" that effectively halted access for any nuclear-powered ships—including US ships—in their ports.[59]

After Lange's remarks, the Reagan administration grew increasingly alarmed at Sagan's efforts. The nuclear winter media campaign began as a battle over public opinion, but it was quickly becoming an issue of national security; gaining support from Hollywood liberals or sympathetic Democrats on the Hill was one thing, but influencing a prime minister to restrict access to ports was a step too far. Lange's decision confirmed the NSC's fears; if other nations followed New Zealand, especially anxious European nations, it might have a domino effect that could damage NATO cohesion. In 1984 these anxieties were warranted, especially as END protests raged. Could Sagan's nuclear winter campaign have a similar effect in Europe? The threat was too serious. Sagan had to be stopped.

The NSC Strikes Back

Sagan had crafted his own media campaign on his own terms, but an uncovered NSC memo reveals that the organization wanted to rein in Sagan by bringing him to "the Hill for further testimony *under oath*"; doing so would provide the government with their "first opportunity for an adversary peer review process since the beginning of this imbroglio." The document's tone is vindictive: "Sagan has much to answer for; his evasion, stonewalling and dissimulation cannot stand a hard cross-examination." The memo also stressed that the NSC "proceed posthaste to poll the nation's atmospheric scientists, most of whom have already caught on to the gap between the [nuclear winter] model and the real world, and publicize their consensus as vigorously as Sagan's sponsors launched his campaign last year." The NSC aimed to deploy "as many of the skeptics . . . as we can" to discredit Sagan. To understand the extent to which nuclear winter threatened US cold war initiatives, consider this lengthy quote from the NSC to defense analyst John M. Fisher:

> The use of Nuclear Winter to justify New Zealand's policy of denying port access to the US Navy's capital ships is just the beginning. The debilitating effect on popular opinion in NATO as well as ANZUS [The Australia, New Zealand, United States Security Treaty of 1951] is potentially devastating. The stakes are already high: the ante by Prime Minister Lange of New Zealand is a million square miles of the Pacific Ocean; that's a pretty big chip for a game in which the dealer is using a stacked deck.
>
> I contend that the worst-case scenario of the Nuclear Winter is actually this: the Nuclear Winter, having become the object of universal popular belief, causes the population of several NATO countries to elect representatives committed to the principal [sic] that the use of theater weapons is to be equated with the end of the world. This might tempt Soviet strategists to conclude that NATO's theater deterrent would not be used and thus lower the threshold for aggression in the event of the Warsaw Pact mobilizing to suppress insurrection in Poland or elsewhere in Eastern Europe. These forces might succumb to the temptation arising from the existing conventional force asymmetry and essay an incursion into NATO territory, precipitating an escalation to theater weapons and beyond. I submit therefore that Dr. Sagan's polemic may be the very disease for which it is presumed to be the cure.[60]

The process of discrediting Sagan was intensive. From 1984 to 1986, he appeared before Congress in four separate hearings, each time expecting to explain the TTAPS findings and their policy implications. The first hearing took place in July 1984, when Sagan appeared alongside Edward Teller before members of the House of Representatives. Both scientists agreed that more work needed to be done on nuclear winter, and despite their differing politics, this agreement made sense. Sagan promoted the nuclear winter theory while Teller supported increased government spending on scientific research. It was a strange setting for a debate over science, but Proxmire had personally called Sagan to speak before his Subcommittee on International Trade,

Finance, and Security Economics of the Joint Economic Committee; Prox-mire supported Sagan and felt the threat of nuclear winter was important. He later submitted S.2693, "Comprehensive Study on Impact of Nuclear Winter," which likely led another senator, William Cohen (R-Maine), to direct the Department of Defense to investigate whether nuclear winter effects should "shape our policy." Thus far, Sagan's appearances before Congress were not as detrimental as the NSC had hoped.[61]

Things got messy when Sagan returned to Washington in mid-July. This time, his policy suggestions for a massive builddown were rebuked by Richard Wagner, a physicist sympathetic to the Reagan administration's arms buildup. Assistant to the secretary of defense for atomic energy, Wagner accused the TTAPS report of being late to the game; the DOD had already investigated nuclear winter–like phenomena through the War College at Maxwell Air Force Base. Regardless, the theory, even if plausible, provided no impetus to change policy—a strong deterrent force remained the best defense.[62] When Proxmire pressed Wagner to elaborate on these findings, he simply repeated that the Reagan administration wished to avoid a nuclear war.

On September 12, 1984, Sagan appeared before the House Committee on Science and Technology's Subcommittee on Natural Resources, Agri-cultural Research, and Environment. He was joined by Stephen Jay Gould, and Edward Teller again provided the counterpoint. Teller argued that while nuclear winter was a serious matter, it did not require any rethinking of defense policy—the numbers simply weren't clear, the computer models too elementary. Input too much soot into the atmosphere, for example, and the computer models actually showed a nuclear warming, not winter. Teller's final remarks were leveled at nuclear winter proponents, who mistakenly "repeated the same calculations with the same assumptions and found the same results, which shows nothing except that our computing machines are working." This, remarked Teller, was "not science; it is a little deviation from ignorance."[63]

Such skepticism was not confined to congressional testimony; similar critiques of the official TTAPS report finally appeared in reputable journals such as *Science, Environment,* and *Nature.* These forums provided (mostly) data-driven criticisms that were somewhat scathing but not outside the realm of scientific peer review, although some comments were more vitriolic than normal. *Nature* editor John Maddox, for example, saw Sagan's publicity campaign as a red flag and noted that it was a shame when "a purportedly sci-entific publication is so fully amplified by popular articles" in *Parade.* It was a line of attack that conservative-leaning media such as the *Wall Street Journal* and the *National Interest* adopted, with both publications calling out Sagan's publicity tactics and media savvy in general as proof that nuclear winter was simply politics disguised as science.[64]

Another wave of backlash came after Sagan submitted an article to the policy journal *Foreign Affairs*. In "Nuclear War and Climatic Catastrophe: Some Policy Implications," Sagan argued that the threat of nuclear winter fundamentally changed the Cold War superpower standoff. The logic was simple: because any nation that engaged in an atomic first strike, even if successful, would itself be destroyed by the resulting global dust cloud, nuclear war had become "tantamount to national suicide for the aggressor—even if the attacked nation" did nothing to retaliate. For Sagan, the conclusion should be obvious: the arms race was pointless, and the only logical way to proceed was with "safe and verifiable reductions of the world strategic inventories to below threshold," or put simply, a 99 percent reduction in global nuclear arms.[65]

Sagan's foray into foreign policy circles was filled with pitfalls, but it did get the government's attention. In March 1985 the Department of Defense released a report on nuclear winter; just a month previous, President Reagan had referred to nuclear winter in a press conference. "They called it [1816] the year in which there was no summer," Reagan remarked (regarding the Tambora explosion). "Now if one volcano can do that, what are we talking about with the whole nuclear exchange, the nuclear winter that scientists had been talking about?"[66] Still, the White House refused to consider Sagan's policy implications; an extreme builddown was out of the question. In a seventeen-page report on the potential effects of nuclear winter, the DOD maintained that "the best way to avoid nuclear winter is to deter nuclear war with present Reagan policies, which includes building new weapons and research on a space based missile shield."[67] Dissenting congressman Timothy Wirth (D-CO) pointed out the obvious—that the threat of nuclear winter should lead to a reduction in nuclear arms, but while Congress agreed with scientists' findings, they also rejected scientists' advice.[68] Wirth was learning just how adept the administration had become in co-opting antinuclear rhetoric to support its policies: "All the Pentagon has done is use this as a soapbox for defending 'Star Wars,'" he correctly concluded.[69]

Similar dismissive arguments appeared in *Foreign Affairs*'s summer 1986 issue, which featured responses to Sagan's previous article demanding a bilateral builddown. In the issue, the strategic theorist Edward Luttwak accused

Sagan of manipulating scientific data to push disarmament, while other critics came to the exact opposite conclusion as Sagan: nuclear winter, with its promise of assured destruction, actually enhanced deterrence. In "Nuclear Winter Reappraised," Starley Thompson and Stephen H. Schneider argued that "on scientific grounds [nuclear winter holds] a vanishingly low level of probability."[70] Such articles show Sagan's inability to sway policymakers, and he would later admit that he "was certainly a novice on issues of strategy."[71]

One article included in *Foreign Affairs* proved especially damning; it was written by Russell Seitz, then director of technology assessment at a Boston banking firm. Seitz was relatively unknown in policy circles, but working in his favor was name recognition—he was the younger cousin of Frederick Seitz, a Princeton University graduate who, after World War II, worked on ballistic missile designs, consulted for the DuPont Corporation, and wrote an influential textbook, *The Modern Theory of Solids*. The elder Seitz later became a NATO science adviser, president of the National Academy of Sciences, and a member of President Nixon's Science Advisory Committee. With his conservative politics and disdain for his liberal colleagues, Seitz found a happy home in the tobacco lobby in 1979, where he worked to discredit science linking tobacco to cancer. In the 1980s, he shifted his focus to Reagan's SDI program, a move that brought him into contact with other conservative scientists, including Edward Teller. This connection to Teller led the elder Seitz to enlist his younger cousin Russell to attack Sagan in *Foreign Affairs*.[72]

Russell Seitz was not a scientist. He had been a visiting scholar at Harvard's Center for International Affairs and had previously worked with the John M. Olin Institute for Strategic Studies, a conservative think tank.[73] TTAPS member O. Brian Toon recalls being baffled at the Seitz article and the author's affiliation: "The byline says he is a Harvard professor, that Harvard is his affiliation. We never heard of Russell Seitz. I had no idea who Russell Seitz was." Toon did some digging and discovered that Seitz was a visiting scholar at Harvard's business school who "attended MIT for a year [and] was a co-author on a paper with somebody who was putting diamond windows on a laser . . . [otherwise] he had no scientific credentials." Despite this questionable background, Seitz confidently criticized the TTAPS report for inaccurate estimates on smoke production and the limitations of Sagan's one-dimensional computer model.[74] Sagan responded with his own accusations, namely that Seitz had borrowed data from other experts, most likely the Lawrence Livermore Laboratory, and that perhaps Seitz was funneled these calculations via his older cousin, who was a friend of Edward Teller. However the data were shared, the American Security Council Foundation (ASCF)—a pro-SDI non-governmental organization based in Cambridge—appropriated Seitz's article to support Reagan administration initiatives and discredit nuclear winter.[75] For groups like the ASCF, data from nonscientists who endorsed SDI proved more appealing than arguments from reputable scientists who discredited "Star Wars."

A similar critique appeared in the *National Review* by another nonscientist, Brad Sparks. Then director of the Political Freedom Fund in Berkeley, Sparks argued that no nuclear winter occurred in the aftermath of Hiroshima or Nagasaki; furthermore, the studies of these bombings never showed any nuclear winter–type effects. To support his claims, he cited "MIT-trained physicist" Russell Seitz. Both men pointed to Sagan's "extraordinary publicity campaign" as proof that Sagan was "artfully constructing the appearance of a consensus" to sell nuclear winter.[76] Another assault came in the fall 1986 issue of the *National Interest,* again from Russel Seitz. "In from the Cold: 'Nuclear Winter' Melts Down" was a scathing attack on the TTAPS predictions which criticized Sagan's publicity campaign and singled out two groups—the Union of Concerned Scientists and Physicians for Social Responsibility—for their roles in funding Sagan's campaign. A similar rebuke came from Howard Maccabee, a past president of Doctors for Disaster Preparedness. In his article "Nuclear Winter: How Much Do We Really Know?" Maccabee called Sagan's "sequence of events—a publicity campaign paid for and launched *before* the publication and circulation of a scientific study—very unusual [and] destructive of the goals of honest inquiry." For critics, then, Sagan's media campaign was evidence of bad science "disguised [for] political purposes."[77]

It was this backlash against Sagan that caught the eye of Reagan's science adviser, George Keyworth, and these critical articles made their way into Keyworth's files.[78] But it's Seitz's original draft for his *National Review* article for the ASCF that made its way to the NSC; titled "The Apocryphal Apocalypse," this seventy-nine-page rambling essay attacks nuclear winter as nothing more than the "confection of media events on or beyond the leading edges of scientific progress." In this document, Seitz accuses the Cornell professor of simply contacting "some childhood friends and political acquaintances, and arranging a gala convocation of octogenarian but spry Nobel Laureates," thereby creating a consensus by which any "scientific impresario can, through the magic of television, conjure up a concrete image in the public's mind of something truly incredible but yet unfalsifiable." Seitz goes on:

If a team of computer programmers and a stable of animators are placed at my disposal, I can give, even-handedly, to advocates and opponents of any controversial subject, environmental, scientific, technical, or strategic, a vivid description of anything their hearts' [sic] desire. To make a stunning impression on the public by showing them a color animation of the ice caps melting in the withering heat of the Nuclear Summer, with the rising sea inundating Washington and Leningrad alike as crops perish in a global drought requires only two things: an utter disregard for science and a few hundred thousand dollars to foot the bill.[79]

"Whence come Dr. Sagan's color slides?" he asked. Hiring artists to represent scientific data irked Seitz; he interviewed Jon Lomberg and Robert Wood, both of whom admitted to "exaggerating the effects" of nuclear winter. However, in a more recent interview, Wood stressed that Seitz took their quotes out of context; additionally, he defended his artistic exaggerations as necessary to make the effects of nuclear winter "more visible." Wood admitted to having moderate politics—he referred to his nuclear winter paintings as strictly "contract work"—but in 1983 he found it impossible to ignore Reagan's arms buildup: "Everybody felt like it was pretty helpless; there was such an arms race, it was a hopeless situation, so no one had ever thought of the ramifications . . . nobody knew about nuclear winter. I was glad to be a part of it." For Seitz, any such admission of exaggeration made it "hard to imagine a more explicit declaration of political intent."[80]

Seitz concluded the report with accusations of conspiracy, claiming that numerous scientists had worked in concert to create the model of nuclear winter for the express purpose of ending the arms race. For Sagan and company to achieve this goal, it was "necessary to transcend the limitations of scientific objectivity and conjure up a new vision of the apocalypse in the popular imagination, [one] so horrifying that a concerted media campaign would . . . induce in the body politic a convulsive rejection of the arsenals of thermonuclear destruction, and precipitate a wholesale reduction in strategic arms by . . . 90 percent."[81]

Clearly, Sagan's one-time use of a public relations firm was coming back to haunt him. Years later, Druyan defended Sagan's efforts and dismissed Seitz's attack: "The work Carl did for nuclear winter was all done without a PR person," she recollected. "People accused him of having some sort of huge PR machine that was generating all this stuff, but it was just us. [Porter Novelli] was only for a specific event, the TTAPS symposium. No one was on retainer, ever." Regardless, for those who supported Reagan's arms buildup, Seitz's accusation that nuclear winter was not science but "a tale of foundation net-working and high stakes grantsmanship [*sic*]" that required "a cashier's check for $80,000 being given to a public relations firm" was all the skepticism they needed.[82]

Seitz lobbed this critique from his new post as the ASCF's "Director of Technology Assessment," a title connoting a full-time position devoted to discrediting scientists and specialists like Sagan whose findings supported disarmament.[83] Seitz wasn't alone in benefiting from Sagan-bashing either; S. Fred Singer also caught the attention of the NSC, especially when he claimed that New Zealand prime minster David Lange's decision to halt US naval ships was "wrong on [*sic*] at least three reasons." Why was Lange in the wrong? First, nuclear-powered vessels were not nuclear bombs; second, the TTAPS nuclear winter findings lacked the credibility that Lange upheld; and third, the PM's decision violated the "traditional right of innocent pas-sage." In Singer's estimation, "freedom of the seas is a fragile concept that needs to be constantly nurtured and protected." It was an odd combination of criticisms: Seitz, the former strategic affairs "expert," had attacked Sagan on ostensibly scientific grounds, while Singer, the scientific "expert," was arguing for the merits of maritime freedom. The label of "expert" seemed to be all one needed to be a credible critic of Sagan—the field of expertise mattered little. By 1985 both Singer and Seitz had the recognition of Keyworth and the ear of the NSC. It was more than enough support; the White House could now cite experts to discredit Sagan.[84] The scientist's crusade to enact policy changes proved ineffectual.

Sagan's nuclear winter campaign did not burn out so much as fade away. Cer-tainly, his extensive efforts to popularize the nuclear winter scenario reached millions of Americans as well as the highest levels of the US and world governments. In 1984, Reagan even remarked that "a great many reputable scientists are telling us that such a war could just end up in no victory for anyone because we would wipe out the earth as we know it."[85] Even if Sagan had reached the president, the administration deftly appropriated the nuclear winter theory to endorse their arms buildup and Reagan's hopes for missile defense. Yet, more than administration efforts diminished nuclear winter's relevance. By 1986, superpower relations improved considerably thanks to the increased communications between Reagan and Soviet premier Mikhail Gorbachev. As atomic tensions abated, the American media largely lost interest in Sagan's apocalyptic predictions.

Still, Sagan continued to promote the nuclear winter hypothesis. In 1990 he and Richard Turco coauthored *A Path Where No Man Thought: Nuclear Winter and the End of the Arms Race,* a 467-page compendium of all nuclear winter research and criticism of the theory to date. In 1991, Sagan reappeared on *Nightline,* where he predicted that the Gulf War oil fires would cause a small-scale nuclear winter in the Middle East. His predictions were off; the oil fires caused only minor and temporary temperature drops. Sagan returned to writing, but after long bouts of illness he died in 1996. In the weeks and months after Sagan's death, national news media bade farewell to the popular scientist. Most neglected to mention his nuclear winter campaign, but not Russell Seitz. In *Forbes Magazine,* Seitz used Sagan's obituary as one last opportunity to attack nuclear winter as scientific alarmism.[86]

Sagan's efforts were not wholly ineffective, however. Because the prospect of nuclear winter alarmed the White House and the NSC, modest funding was allocated to studying the possible phenomenon. Still, Sagan's use of American mass media was a pivotal decision, one that may have helped him to popularize nuclear winter but also opened him to criticism from conservative commentators. His hiring of a public relations firm, his oversight of the creation of media aids, and his extensive involvement in a media campaign allowed nonscientists to attack Sagan. In transcending traditional peer-review methods and spreading warnings in American popular media, Sagan was simply doing what he did best: make science accessible to the general public. It was a crucial decision, one that put Sagan on the defensive against critics sympathetic to Reagan's arms initiatives.

Sagan's nuclear winter campaign remains an important part of 1980s Cold War history, especially after it helped convince David Lange to block US naval vessels from using New Zealand ports. Additionally, the threat of nuclear winter may have alarmed the Soviets far more than American policymakers. According to Druyan, the distinguished cosmonaut Alexei Layanoff believed that Sagan's remarks to Soviet leaders left an impression, especially on Mikhail Gorbachev. Layanoff recalled that after "Carl left the room— giving the nuclear winter story to Gorbachev and the central committee— they looked at each other and said, 'Well, it's over, isn't it?'"[87] At the same time, Soviet dissidents who promoted the nuclear winter theory ended up in jail. Still, for a Soviet leader seeking to limit defense expenditures and fix a teetering economy, a scientific theory calling the expensive arms race futile must have had big appeal. In 2000, Gorbachev recalled that in the 1980s, "models made by Russian and American scientists showed that a nuclear war would result in a nuclear winter that would be extremely destructive to all life on Earth; the knowledge of that was a great stimulus to us, the people of honor and morality, to act in that situation."[88]

In the short run, however, the Reagan administration successfully contained Sagan's nuclear winter campaign. As Badash notes, Sagan's "congressional hearings on NW seemed to result in little. Aside from requiring the secretary of defense to prepare a few annual reports on the phenomenon, no legislation emerged, nor did the administration act on requests for joint research with Soviet scientists."[89] The nuclear winter story, then, shows that the Reagan administration could not ignore efforts of concerned cultural activists, but became adept at co-opting rhetoric of dissent to support their own arms initiatives. Another challenge to those initiatives came in November 1983, when the White House struggled to contain the biggest antinuclear media event of the decade: ABC's film *The Day After.*

3

Containing *The Day After*

By the time it aired on Sunday, November 20, 1983, ABC's apocalyptic drama *The Day After* had already become a nationwide media event. The buzz about the film was intense thanks to its timeliness, airing after six tumultuous months of steadily deteriorating superpower relations. Beginning in March 1983, President Reagan's rhetoric, notably his "Evil Empire" and Strategic Defense Initiative speeches alarmed peace activists at home and concerned leaders abroad. Reagan's adventurism overseas was equally disquieting. In addition to continued covert operations in Afghanistan, the president had committed a small "peacekeeping" force to Beirut. Convinced that eight hundred US Marines would help stabilize the region and prevent an Israeli invasion of Lebanon, Reagan was tragically proven wrong when, in April, terrorists bombed the US embassy, taking seventeen American lives.

Tensions escalated further on September 1, 1983, when Soviet military aircraft shot down Korean Airliner 007, killing of 269 civilians—including 61 Americans and US Representative Lawrence McDonald (who was a member of the conservative John Birch Society). Privately, Reagan urged restraint, but publicly the president called the act a "crime against humanity." In the days that followed, Moscow refused to accept responsibility. Andrei Gromyko offered only that "the world situation is now slipping toward a very danger-ous precipice." Looking back, Reagan biographer Lou Cannon reflected that by September 1983, the global situation had "gone beyond words."[1] October proved even more precipitous. On October 23, 1983, a suicide bomber drove an explosive-packed delivery van past the gates and into an American military barracks in Lebanon. The blast, then the largest non-nuclear explosion on record, killed 241 US Marines; two days later, Reagan sent troops to Grenada.[2]

October also marked the impending importation of American nuclear warheads into Western Europe. The Euromissile crisis began in 1977 with President Carter's response to the Soviet deployment of SS-20 intermediate-range ballistic missiles (IRBMs) throughout the Eastern Bloc. The SS-20's MIRV design threatened to destabilize the European theater by tripling the atomic payload of each Soviet missile. Alarmed, West German chancellor Helmut Schmidt asked for support, and in 1979 NATO proposed a "dual track" response. On one track, the United States promised to deploy Pershing II IRBMs and tactical cruise missiles throughout Great Britain, Italy, and West Germany by 1983; on the other track, it would negotiate for the removal of SS-20s that threatened Europe. In 1981, Carter's decision became Reagan's burden, and the administration's "Zero Option" proposal proved to be one of the White House's most controversial foreign policy issues. Its architect, Richard Perle, was a protégé of the nuclear strategist Albert Wohlstetter, a hawkish conservative; Perle did not trust, or likely did not want to negotiate with, the Soviets. Basically, with the Zero Option he was asking something (Soviet disarmament) for nothing (*not* deploying American missiles), and Perle's gambit has been assessed by some as a strategy designed to fail.[3] Not surprisingly, the Soviets refused this offer, and as the Euromissile deployment approached, antinuclear protests sprang up in Great Britain, France, and West Germany.[4]

Considering this context, it's hard to imagine a more frightening time for ABC to air *The Day After,* especially because its plot seemed based on real geopolitical events. In the film, nuclear war breaks out after American–Soviet confrontation in Europe, a narrative eerily mimicking the recent Euromissile deployment. Because of the similarity and because it aired at a tense time, pundits estimated that one hundred million Americans would tune in, turning *The Day After* into the most widely watched media event of the year.[5]

The film can hardly be called high art and is at times heavy-handed in conveying its antinuclear message. Set in Lawrence, Kansas, and nearby Kansas City, Missouri, it's a story about ordinary Americans—farmers, doctors, students, soldiers—who survive an atomic attack only to perish from radioactive fallout and societal breakdown. The first half of the film focuses on the banality of American life, juxtaposing daily routine with in-scene commentary (usually as television and radio broadcasts) explaining military escalations overseas. Frequently, characters expound on issues ranging from the 1962 Cuban missile crisis to the dangers of nuclear weapons, electromagnetic pulses, and radioactivity. The film's second half, by contrast, is more dire.

About an hour into the film, midwestern weapon silos open, ICBMs launch, and panic ensues. As the masses scramble for cover, Lawrence and Kansas City are obliterated. What follows is a not-so-subtle message: there's no surviving a nuclear war. Whatever its merits as a film, *The Day After* stands as the starkest dramatization of nuclear war ever shown on American television.[6]

Because of when it aired and the hype it created, *The Day After* was more than an antinuclear film; it became a nationwide media event, one that brought the nuclear debate into millions of American homes. The *New York Times* critic John Corry mused that "ABC's much-discussed vision of nuclear Armageddon is no longer only a television film: it has become an event, a rally and a controversy, much of it orchestrated." The White House agreed. In a memo to Edwin Meese, Special Assistant for Policy Information Kevin R. Hopkins expressed his concerns: "I had the privilege yesterday of viewing the upcoming ABC-TV film *The Day After* and found it both well-done and powerful. I am all the more convinced that this film could have a significant effect on public opinion, and that an appropriate posture on our part is imperative in order to minimize any damage and/or take advantage of the film to promote our country's national security interests."[7] Clearly, the White House recognized the potential of this "orchestrated" antinuclear event to galvanize public opinion against the arms race. It had to respond.

Creating *The Day After*

The Day After was the brainchild of ABC Motion Pictures president Brandon Stoddard. In 1977, Stoddard produced the miniseries *Roots,* a popular adaptation of Alex Haley's 1976 novel about American slavery. The series was so successful that Stoddard looked for new, equally provocative material. After seeing *The China Syndrome,* a movie about the dangers of nuclear power, he decided to create his own antinuclear film, this time about the dangers of nuclear weapons. He enlisted the screenwriter Edward Hume, who prepared for the assignment by scouring government civil defense literature. Hume hoped to use official government language from civil defense propaganda to show the American public a realistic representation of nuclear war's devastating effects on society. Admittedly "sympathetic with disarmament," Hume agreed to do the project because he was growing increasingly "alarmed by the state of [US] defense policy" under President Reagan.[8]

With his screenwriter on board, Stoddard now needed a director. After three invitations were declined (citing the film as too depressing), Stoddard's fourth choice, Nicholas Meyer, accepted. By 1983, Meyer had made a name for himself both as a writer, especially for his novel-turned-screenplay *The Seven-Percent Solution,* and as a director, notably of two successful *Star Trek* movies. Meyer agreed to work on *The Day After* out of a sense of duty. "I didn't want to make this movie," he told the *Washington Post.* "I did it to be a Boy Scout, to do my good deed for the day. I did this to be a good citizen. I thought it was a civic responsibility." Sympathetic with disarmament, Meyer hoped that *The Day After* would stimulate public dialogue about nuclear war among apathetic Americans: "I did not want to preach to the converted," he admitted; instead, he and ABC were "going after those who haven't formed an opinion."[9] It was a lofty goal, considering that previous Cold War atomic films statistically had done little to convert citizens into antinuclear activists. In the early 1980s, however, there were hints that atomic films were capturing the public's imagination. For instance, in 1982 *The Atomic Café,* a sardonic look at 1950s US civil defense propaganda, became popular on college campuses; other antinuclear films, such as *Threads* and *Testament,* were already in production. Because it promised an unflinching view of the horrors of nuclear war after six months of deteriorating superpower relations, *The Day After* held the potential to garner a huge audience.[10]

Meyer worked to make *The Day After* as realistic as possible. For research, he read Jonathan Schell's *The Fate of the Earth,* examined US civil defense plans, and studied nuclear phenomena such as electromagnetic pulses (EMPs). He hoped to juxtapose realistic and frightening aspects of nuclear war with the banality of middle American life.[11] If he drove home the impossibility of surviving a nuclear war, Meyer could call out the Reagan administration—those who had bragged about winning a nuclear war just a year previous—as liars. Often, the director towed ABC's line of nonpartisanship, stating that *The Day After* was not political and not meant to support disarmament. Other times, he was more forthright, even stating that he hoped to "sober the world and slow the pace with which we seem determined to turn our planet into a nuclear porcupine" and, ultimately, "clobber sixty million people over the head" with an antinuclear message.[12] That was a conservative estimate, and Meyer exceeded his goal by forty million. If gauged in terms of ratings, popularity, and news coverage, *The Day After* and its estimated one hundred million viewers makes it one of the most-watched media events of the 1980s.[13]

As its airdate approached, conservative critics who had previewed the film panned it as antinuclear propaganda, but Meyer did little to deflect the criticism. Publicly, he maintained that his film was "fiction based on fact," and *The Day After* opened with a disclaimer: "Although based on scientific fact, the following film is fiction." On October 13, some five weeks before it aired, Meyer stated on National Public Radio that *The Day After* was a "public service announcement" and that he was elated that ABC was "spending millions of dollars to go on the air and call Ronald Reagan a liar."[14] In response, Reagan supporters quickly labeled the film subjective propaganda against the arms buildup. William F. Buckley's *National Review* sarcastically suggested that *The Day After* was a film "for all of you who thought nuclear war would be a piece of cake," while the *New York Post* asked: "Why is Nicholas Meyer doing Yuri Andropov's job?"[15] Such reviews, printed even before the film had aired, hinted at how divisive *The Day After* would become.

The criticisms only added to the film's buzz, however, and soon antinuclear organizations were using *The Day After* as a cause for new antinuclear events. Roger Molander's Ground Zero group distributed 200,000 viewing guides that encouraged "people to watch the film in groups and join the [antinuclear] movement" while the Campaign against Nuclear War scheduled two days of disarmament seminars to coincide with the film.[16] Other groups established toll-free telephone hotlines that concerned citizens could call to join their organizations. Anticipating a strong response, ABC executives established their own phone counseling hotline; so did the White House. As early as September, viewers had hints of how dire ABC's film would be, especially after a *New York Times* editorial called it "relentlessly depressing, with scenes of enormous destruction by firestorm, people being vaporized, mass graves, the irretrievable loss of food and water supplies, vandalism and murder, the breakdown of medical care and disfigurement and death from radiation sickness."[17] By late October 1983, *The Day After* was eliciting similar reviews across the nation. Newspaper ads called the film a "starkly realistic drama of nuclear confrontation and its devastating effects on a group of average American citizens." Few made-for-television films had ever garnered such a response, leading the critic Edward Gorman to call *The Day After* "the most powerful use of TV in American history."[18]

The film was powerful because it conjured comparisons to real-world geopolitical events. Citing the recent KAL 007 shoot down, the *National Review* asserted that Meyer's film actually supported deterrence: "The producers at ABC obviously want to impress upon us just what might happen if our deterrent becomes unconvincing, tempting the Soviets to treat Lawrence, Kansas, as if it were a Korean airplane." Recalling the Euromissile protests, the *Washington Times* believed that the film would bring "joy to the hearts of the advocates of nuclear freeze and other anti-nuke types on the eve of the deployment of Pershing II and cruise missiles in Western Europe." SDI supporters High Frontier proposed that *The Day After* "and media coverage of it, would seem to increase the distance, and the level of feelings, between the anti-nuke and the pro-defense factions." If Meyer hoped that his film would spark public dialogue, he certainly achieved that goal.[19]

ABC was more than happy to fuel such debate. They distributed more than half a million "viewer's guides" to spark conversation, purchased full-page advertisements—such as "The Day After: Beyond Imagining," which included images of an American family watching ICBMs fly out of underground silos nestled in Kansas cornfields—and scheduled accompanying programs for a full week of antinuclear television.[20] One such program, *War Games,* would be a week-long series that showed the actual "decision making tactics in government crisis management [that are] designed to prevent escalation and confrontation." Later aired as *The Crisis Game,* it included commentary from former defense secretary Clark Clifford, the noted diplomat Richard Holbrooke, the historian and JFK adviser Arthur Schlesinger, former assistant secretary of state Leslie Gelb, and the Harvard historian Richard Pipes.[21]

All of this publicity leading up to *The Day After* did not surprise the Reagan administration. In fact, as the buzz grew, the White House was working on a preemptive media blitz, one that could capitalize on *The Day After*'s hype to publicize a new, peaceful rhetoric and co-opt Meyer's message about the futility of nuclear war.

The White House Preempts

The administration's efforts to contain Meyer's two-hour antinuclear "public service announcement" started in the Pentagon, which had initially allowed ABC access to airbases and equipment for the film. They reconsidered such access after learning that Meyer would insinuate that the United States, not the Soviet Union, instigated the film's nuclear apocalypse. When the Department of Defense demanded that the script be changed to blame the Russians, Meyer refused, and the Pentagon retracted ABC's access to US Air Force bases. It was only after Assistant to the President for Communications David Gergen pressed the issue that ABC ultimately acquiesced, making the film's final cut ambiguous as to which superpower launched first.[22] But this was just the beginning; by November 9, internal White House memoranda trace a coordinated, detailed, and sweeping public affairs plan to contain the potentially critical fallout from *The Day After*. Specifically, drafts of this plan made clear: "The aim will be to channel peoples' [*sic*] emotional reactions to the film into support for the President's efforts to strengthen deterrence and reduce the threat of nuclear war."[23] It was an audacious political pivot. This is how they executed it.

On November 9, 1983, Robert Sims, then special assistant to the president and senior director of public affairs on the National Security Council, advised National Security Advisor Robert C. "Bud" McFarlane and David Gergen of the following actions. First, the NSC should distribute "talking points" to "all Administration spokesmen" to prepare them to defend "the President's policies of deterrence and arms control." These talking points were to be sent to "several hundred Administration appointees" as well as "a small number" of influential "conservative columnists." Sims tasked Karna Small-Stringer, director of the recently formed Office of Media Relations, with contacting "Conservative Columnists and Commentators" for support. Simultaneously, the NSC would prepare a "White House Digest" publication to outline the president's views on arms control for the press, as well as a question-and-answer guide laying out "the best ways to respond to the film or questions raised by the public or media" to be made available to "all Base Commanders, defense agencies and Public Affairs Officers world-wide." Finally, a "rotary hot-line" was set up for "mid-level specialists at the Department of Defense to answer requests from local radio and TV talk shows." Clearly, the NSC wanted everyone from high-ranking officials to low-level staffers equipped to serve as impromptu spokespeople who could defend the president's policies in the wake of *The Day After*.[24]

Two days later, with only nine days until *The Day After's* broadcast, President Reagan was in Japan attending a World War Two commemoration. Now peaceful allies, these former advisories shared a unique past: Japan remained the only nation ever attacked with atomic weapons, and the United States the only nation to use them in wartime. For this reason, and in the wake of rising Cold War atomic fears, the press would be closely following Reagan's remarks that day. It was a unique opportunity in a tense time, and the administration aimed to jettison its previous rhetoric about fighting and winning a nuclear war and assume a more conciliatory tone. Appropriately, it was Veteran's Day, and Reagan delivered. One part of his speech became especially important in the days leading up to *The Day After*:

Armed with these materials, congressional district chairmen were to begin calling ABC affiliates to "express concern over the content and timing of the film [as well as] ask them for time to air an editorial response to the film." Their goal was explicit: to "call every television and radio station in their district and ask what talk shows will be discussing" the film, contact "newspapers and offer to write a guest editorial on the subject of strategic defense," and paint the film as propaganda presented "without regard to facts or responsible judgment." Overall, the CFA succeeded in coordinating 110 pro-administration press releases set to appear the morning of Monday, November 21—the day after *The Day After*.[38]

The administration's most fervent source of outside support, however, came from Daniel Graham's High Frontier organization. Graham, who would lead a zealous pro-SDI media campaign (the focus of chapter 4), anticipated a considerable backlash from *The Day After* and was wary that "nuclear freeze groups" would try to "capitalize on public sentiment generated by the film to renew a push for a freeze resolution in Congress." High Frontier crafted its own public relations plan which, like the White House plan, was "not designed to debate the film's accuracy or to deny in any way the horror of nuclear war," but instead provide "a means by which the Administration can express its views" and "calm . . . public fears." High Frontier hoped to "channel peoples' [*sic*] emotional reactions to the film into support for the President's efforts to strengthen deterrence."[39]

On November 4, 1983, Graham mailed his plans to numerous White House officials in a lengthy document titled "High Frontier: Two Day Media Blitz." In it, Graham expressed concerns that the "pro-freeze film has already stirred a storm of anti-nuclear sentiment across the country." Because it was "expected to draw a 50 share [*sic*] of the audience," and become one of the "highest rated shows of all time," High Frontier wanted to run pro-administration ads during commercial breaks. Graham exhorted the White House not to "allow the disarmament lobby to capitalize on this emotional movie [and] play on the fears and frustrations of the citizens of this country." To help, High Frontier advertisements would "provide a sensible alternative" to blind disarmament.[40]

Graham's "media blitz" proposed full-page ads in major newspapers, including the *Washington Post, Miami Herald, San Diego Union Tribune, Topeka Capital Journal, Denver Post,* and *New York Times,* as well as television ads to air during the Ted Koppel *Viewpoint* special and on numerous local affiliates. That kind of media presence did not come cheap, and High Frontier simply did not "have the financial resources on hand to purchase this time." So, Graham asked the White House to contact wealthy conservatives, such as Joseph Coors and W. Clement Stone, and solicit donations of $500,000 from each for High Frontier's efforts.[41]

The White House rejected Graham's request, and cautioned administration officials "not to become involved" with fundraising for High Frontier because "as a general principle, such activities are better handled outside the White House." Not wanting to dismay one of their strongest supporters, however, officials later reassured Graham that President Reagan remained "deeply committed" to SDI and that he would follow High Frontier's efforts with great interest. Despite this setback, High Frontier put together enough money to film its own pro-missile defense documentary that aired the week following *The Day After*. While some forty ABC affiliates aired the pro-defense special, the White House's reluctance to aid Graham hinted at future administration efforts to distance themselves from him and his zealous SDI supporters.[42]

By November 18, just two days before its airdate, television pundits speculated on what, if any, role *The Day After* might have on the antinuclear movement. CBS's Bill Moyers argued that if the film had any power, it was because it "contradicts our basic American optimism that everything has a happy ending, even a confrontation between superpowers. It confounds the idea of American Exceptionalism." On ABC, news anchor Peter Jennings offered that "*The Day After* has become a political tool [and] conservatives are concerned that it will play into the hands of the anti-nuclear movement." The evangelical leader Jerry Falwell, a longtime Reagan supporter, dismissed the film's message and commented that "one can think of no other subject from foreign policy to the economy that a network would dare to present in such a one dimensional manner." Congressman Vin Weber (R-MN) criticized the film as an attempt to remove tactical nuclear missiles from the European theater.[43]

The most common criticism on network news, however, was one that the White House specifically requested its conservative commentators share: that the film might traumatize children. It was a sound strategy, as even those who supported the film's antinuclear message believed that children should not view it without parental supervision; others argued that because of the film's graphic nature, children not be allowed to watch it at all. One CBS news broadcast from Lawrence, Kansas, featured a preacher exclaiming, "Let's reject the vision of *The Day After*. Let's reject it! Let's reject it for us and let's reject its despair and doom and gloom for our children." In the same broadcast, a local resident advised children not to worry about nuclear war because "adults are working on that. You don't need to worry about that." White House talking points had shaped the dynamics of televised debates regarding *The Day After.*[44]

On November 20, just minutes before broadcast, White House officials made their final push on network news. Ken Adelman appeared on CBS to argue that *The Day After*'s premise was flawed, that worrying "about a nuclear conflict the day after is useless; it's managing to prevent one the day before that counts. That's the real message of tonight's television movie."[45] Adelman's remarks summed up a concerted White House effort, one that utilized top-ranking cabinet members, sympathetic pundits and columnists, NGOs, and a multitude of print, radio, and televised media, to sway millions of Americans to be wary of the film's antinuclear message. The Reagan administration had done what Kevin Hopkins had hoped: not attack the film on technical grounds or shy away from it but instead "view it as an opportunity to make our case" and "talk constructively about how to prevent" nuclear war.[46] In only a few weeks, the administration had turned a potentially damaging media event into a platform to change its rhetoric. The spin would continue after *The Day After*'s final credits rolled.

ABC's *Viewpoint*

Immediately following the film, ABC aired *Viewpoint,* a news special featuring anchorman Ted Koppel, who moderated a nuclear-themed roundtable discussion unlike any other in television history. After highlighting the importance of the film ("much more than a movie; it has become a national event"), Koppel introduced his panel, which included William F. Buckley Jr., the writer and Holocaust survivor Elie Wiesel, former secretary of defense Robert S. McNamara, former national security adviser and secretary of state Henry Kissinger, former national security adviser (and chairman of President Reagan's bipartisan commission on the MX missile) Brent Scowcroft, Carl Sagan, and finally—and perhaps most important—Secretary of State George Shultz.

The choice of Shultz to represent the White House was made after much debate. As early as October 7, ABC requested that Vice President Bush comment on the film, and that UN ambassador Jeane Kirkpatrick join the roundtable discussion; but neither Bush, who had previously bragged about

American nuclear superiority, nor Kirkpatrick, whose rigid foreign policy opinions—famously expressed in her 1979 *Commentary* article "Dictator-ships and Double Standards"—were ideal representatives to tout a new, mod-erate line. For this particular public affairs strategy, Shultz was a perfect fit. A pragmatist, Shultz played a vital role in transitioning Reagan's foreign policy away from the hardline stances of Pipes, Weinberger, and Perle, and toward reopening talks with the Soviets. To minimize his participation, the secretary of state opted to attend remotely, via closed circuit—a calculated move that ensured a limited time commitment and, it was hoped, would avoid a poten-tially dangerous free-flowing discussion.[47]

Viewpoint opened on a somber tone. After introducing the participants, Koppel reassured the millions of viewers that "we're all still here," that "what we have all just seen" was not reality but a frightening possibility in a nuclear world. Next, he wondered whether "the vision that we've just seen [is] the future as it will be or the future as it may be? Is there still time?" He aimed the question directly at Shultz, who reassured viewers that *The Day After* did not depict the future; it only provided a "vivid and dramatic portrayal of the fact that nuclear war is simply not acceptable." These remarks were straight from the "Public Affairs Strategy" playbook, as was Shultz's claim that avoiding nuclear war "has been the policy of the United States for decades now—the successful policy of the United States. We simply do not accept nuclear war, and we have been successful in preventing it."[48]

Koppel knew that the secretary of state was reciting a script; indeed, viewers at home likely recognized that Shultz was reading cue cards. So, he restated the question: How would Shultz respond if, instead of addressing millions of Americans, he had to explain to a close family member Ameri-ca's arms buildup? Shultz didn't flinch; he stuck to the talking points: "The only reason that we have nuclear weapons, as President Reagan said in Japan recently, is to see to it that they are not used." Additionally, the president was already working to "reduce the number of nuclear weapons" in the world; since the 1960s the total US nuclear destructive power had been reduced by 70 percent. Reagan wanted to remove nuclear warheads from Europe, so, if Americans could take anything valuable away from *The Day After*, it was the "unacceptability of nuclear warfare. It says to those who have criticized the President for seeking reductions—that really is the sensible course to take. We should be rallying around and supporting . . . the idea that we should be reducing the numbers of these weapons." In only five minutes, Shultz had crisply mentioned nearly all of the White House's prepared talking points; in doing so, he successfully pivoted Koppel's questions to emphasize Reagan's hopes for peace.

After Shultz, the discussion turned to the roundtable. Buckley called the film communist propaganda—"the whole point of this movie is to launch an enterprise that seeks to debilitate the United States"—and accused Brandon Stoddard of creating a pro-nuclear freeze film that, if effective in compelling Americans to join the antinuclear cause, would only weaken the United States. Carl Sagan disagreed. He applauded ABC for "spurring what I hope will be a yearlong debate" on the nuclear arms race. Then, after explaining the new scientific theory of nuclear winter, he criticized Reagan's SDI program. Specifically, Sagan questioned Shultz's estimation that the White House was reducing the number of global nuclear weapons, rebutting that instead "what the administration is really doing—according to the congressional budget office—is increasing the inventory of strategic warheads from nine thousand in the United States to fourteen thousand." Sagan also responded to an audience question regarding the plausibility of the nuclear freeze movement. He stressed that the freeze was "a good first step," but then summarized the global nuclear situation with an analogy: "A room, awash in gasoline, and there are two implacable enemies in that room. One of them has nine thousand matches; the other has seven thousand matches. Each of them is concerned about who's ahead, who's stronger. Well, that's the kind of situation that we are actually in . . . What is necessary is to reduce the matches and to clean up the gasoline."

The discussion continued with Kissinger, who argued that *The Day After* had oversimplified a complex issue, and that instead of engaging "in an orgy of demonstrating how terrible the causalities of a nuclear war are," policymakers should focus on how to avoid a nuclear war. McNamara concurred, and praised the film because he did "not believe that the American people understand the world we live in [nor the] risk we face." The former secretary of defense, who had helped JFK navigate the Cuban missile crisis, offered specifics: "There are forty thousand nuclear warheads in the inventories of the United States and the Soviet Union today, with the destructive power roughly a million times that of the Hiroshima bomb. I don't know any arms expert, and I doubt that at anyone in this room believes, that in the next ten to fifteen years we can reduce that number by more than half." Scowcroft followed by endorsing a US "military posture which the Soviets—whatever they think about deterrence, when they think about the nature of nuclear weapons—can never imagine that to resort to them makes sense." Finally, Elie Wiesel urged that Americans not see *The Day After*'s events as an impossible tragedy; he reminded viewers that the tragedy of the Holocaust, in which millions of innocents needlessly died, had already happened.

Koppel then turned to the studio audience for questions. When asked about the feasibility of space-based defenses (such as SDI), Kissinger expressed doubt about any technological fix to the Cold War standoff. When Koppel asked Sagan to respond to this same question, he scoffed at Reagan's SDI program and argued that any "ballistic missile defense system . . . is dangerous because it lulls us into thinking that we can get away from this problem." McNamara urged that the Reagan administration renounce the idea of "launch on warning" and instead propose a policy of No First Use; Scowcroft supported peace through strength; Wiesel shared optimism about human rights and antinuclear movements in Russia; Buckley stressed the need to flex American military muscle to deter a Soviet first strike; Sagan concluded, "I think that this can be done, we can get out of this trap that we and the Soviets have jointly set for ourselves and our civilization and our species but the way to cut nuclear weapons is to cut nuclear weapons." Koppel ended the program by applauding *The Day After* for shaking up national complacency toward nuclear weapons.

On November 21, the morning after *The Day After,* the media began assessing the film and what, if any, effect it would have on the public. One reviewer deemed the film important because it "removes the unimaginable from the abstract and makes it shatteringly real: this is what a nuclear Armageddon is going to look like."[49] Some attention fell on the residents of Lawrence, Kansas, many of whom acted as extras in *The Day After.* One NBC report featured footage from a conservative rally in which participants burned a Soviet flag while a young man denounced freeze activists and promised that he was not "just going to wait around until the communists get strong enough and then surrender." ABC covered a second rally, during which a local resident called the film a "two-and-a-half-hour commercial for the Kremlin, and they didn't even have to put KGB actors in it." Another Lawrence resident called the film "Communist propaganda." Nicholas Meyer may have succeeded in bringing the nuclear debate to Middle America, but the film was clearly polarizing.[50]

After weeks of planning and days of efforts, David Gergen informed the president that "activities relating to *The Day After*" were highly effective. "Our administration spokesmen (and women) have done a first rate job over the past few days in promoting your policies during the renewed debate over nuclear arms." He especially applauded Shultz's performance as "particularly effective in framing the issue [of] (how do we prevent a nuclear holocaust?) and in providing the answer (support your policies of deterrence and arms reduction)." Gergen saw these remarks as vital in helping the White House take "the lead" in nationwide nuclear debates. Altogether, *The Day After*, a film created to spark antinuclear debate, had instead, after this media campaign, resulted in a large public show of support for the president and his policies.[51]

Gergen was relying on polling and survey data taken in the wake of *The Day After* which showed little change in public perceptions of nuclear war. One Warner–Amex Qube cable network poll found "no dramatic shift one way or the other in the opinions of those who viewed" *The Day After*.[52] Another survey found that for most viewers largely "no change occurred in views on the likelihood of nuclear war" and that "most people [remained] pessimistic about the chances of their surviving a nuclear war both before and after the movie." The survey also found that "there was no political fallout from the movie among average viewers [and that] defense and arms control issues showed no movement among those who had just seen *The Day After*," and while 78 percent of viewers supported a nuclear freeze when the antinuclear film aired, "President Reagan suffered no damage from the movie." These are not so much indictments on *The Day After's* potential to sway public opinion but instead, as Gergen assessed in late November 1983, a positive appraisal of the White House's highly effective media offensive.[53]

After the Reagan Presidency, historians sympathetic to Reagan's Cold War policies cite these polls and similar data as proof that Americans were not as concerned about nuclear war as some peace scholars have argued. Others assert that *The Day After* failed to sway Americans because it presented a one-dimensional take on the complex issue of nuclear strategy.[54] Such conclusions discount the considerable efforts the Reagan administration undertook to contain the potentially damaging aftereffects of this film. These efforts turned *The Day After*, a film created to challenge the arms buildup, into an opportunity to promote the president's new goal of preventing—not prevailing in—a nuclear war.

The broadcast of *The Day After* contributed to an important period of the Reagan administration. Late October 1983 until March 1984 is sometimes seen as a time of "reversal" in Reagan's thinking, the beginning of a new era of rapprochement with the Soviets. To be sure, in the months that followed *The Day After*, Shultz reengaged with the Soviets and influenced Reagan to do the same. With the death in 1985 of Konstantin Chernenko, Mikhail Gorbachev assumed power, instituted the policies of *glastnost* and *perestroika*, and helped to transform Soviet society. In the realm of public perception, however, the efforts to contain the political fallout from *The Day After* had a lasting effect. Before *The Day After* aired, many Americans were unsure that Reagan sought to avoid nuclear conflict; afterward, tens of millions of Americans were reassured of his commitment to prevent such a war from ever happening.[55]

Largely, this trend of easing tensions continued, especially after the nuclear summits between Reagan and Gorbachev that would ultimately lead to actual nuclear arms reductions in Europe. That process, however, was not easy or immediate, and the biggest roadblock to achieving these breakthroughs would be Reagan's Strategic Defense Initiative. But SDI wasn't simply an impediment at the negotiating table. After *The Day After*, Reagan's dream of space-based missile defense became the focal point of another, prolonged publicity battle that challenged the administration in mass media.

4

Weapons in Space

In March 1983, Gallup poll numbers indicated that Ronald Reagan's reelection remained uncertain. By January 1983, the president's approval ratings had plummeted to 35 percent. It was an alarming drop from May 1981, when Reagan's ratings peaked at 68 percent after the failed assassination attempt by John Hinckley.[1] For a time, the attempt had made the president hugely popular and helped him pass sweeping tax cuts, the cornerstone of an economic program that would later be labeled Reaganomics. But in early 1983, the unavoidable fact was that, despite promises that these cuts would benefit everyone, America's economy lingered in recession, with 9.8 percent of the workforce unemployed.[2] Additionally, after the White House's "Peaceful Offensive," which had done much to discredit freeze resolutions in state referenda, the nuclear freeze campaign was still very active.

As he waited for the economy to rebound, Reagan sought to regain support from his evangelical base, many of whom were gravitating toward the calls for peace of the freeze campaign. To do so, he addressed a group in Orlando, Florida, with a speech that became one of the defining statements of his presidency—the "Evil Empire" speech. In it, Reagan accused the Soviets of being the "focus of evil" in the modern world. He exhorted his evangelical base to reject the temptation of the freeze and stand strong with his arms initiatives. With this speech, Reagan hoped to regain the moral high ground in the arms race debates, reaffirm his evangelical base, and slow the freeze campaign's momentum. Retrospectively, admirers see Reagan's rhetoric as proof of his genuine hardline stance against communism, but at the time the speech alarmed antinuclear groups and the Soviet politburo.

Even after the speech, Reagan's approval ratings remained low. What he needed was a game changer, a political maneuver that could halt the freeze movement's momentum, co-opt its peaceful message, and transform his image from a warmonger to a peacekeeper. On March 23, 1983, he accomplished all three goals in a single televised address. To a national audience, the president shared his hope that instead of the long-standing Cold War threat of Mutually Assured Destruction, the United States might someday successfully defend itself against nuclear attack. Reagan expressed his faith that the American "scientific community . . . those that gave us nuclear weapons," might one day build a system to render those weapons "impotent and obsolete." Thus, from his own hopes and dreams—and against numerous advisers' warnings—Reagan singlehandedly launched the Strategic Defense Initiative.[3]

SDI remains one of the most curious political developments of the 1980s, and more than thirty years later, historians continue to debate SDI's potential and its role in Reagan's presidency. Sympathetic scholars see SDI as part of Reagan's Cold War strategy to spend the Soviets into submission, a form of economic warfare. Skeptics view "Star Wars" as an unachievable program, a boondoggle that impeded nuclear abolition and prolonged poor superpower relations. Others see SDI as part of Reagan's rhetorical rearmament, a deft political calculation to halt the momentum of the freeze movement. Regardless of interpretation, Star Wars remains a major component of the Reagan administration's legacy. In launching SDI, Reagan ignored his cabinet's concerns that a space-based defense system against ICBMs threatened the logic of Cold War deterrence. For this reason, SDI contributed to Cold War tensions, and helped to make 1983 the tensest year since 1962 and the Cuban missile crisis. Understandably, SDI is considered one of the most unexpected, important, and polarizing announcements of Reagan's presidency.[4]

Opposition to SDI arose almost immediately. Some of Reagan's most vocal critics were scientists, the very group he asked to create a program that could render nuclear weapons "impotent and obsolete." Many in the scientific community, especially members of the Union of Concerned Scientists, worked hard to discredit SDI. Led by the MIT physicist Henry Kendall and Carl Sagan, from 1983 to 1986 the UCS tried to convince the American public that Star Wars was a dangerous dream. "Few American scientists believe Star Wars can do what the President hopes," the UCS argued; they saw SDI as an unattainable program, one that would only distract citizens from an ongoing and dangerous nuclear arms race. Even if Reagan's dream could be achieved, it would only give the United States a first-strike capability, and doing so might embolden policymakers who had long bragged about winning a nuclear war to actually start one. SDI, then, actually promised to escalate an arms race already spiraling out of control. Sympathetic philanthropists, including members of the Rockefeller family, agreed with this assessment and funneled millions of dollars into the UCS's anti-SDI media campaign.[5]

As the UCS rallied against Star Wars in the mass media, Daniel Graham's High Frontier organization was busy creating books, television ads, documentary films, and innovative direct mail pieces aimed at raising public awareness of and support for missile defense. In time, Graham came to believe that his media battle with the UCS would be vital to SDI's success: "Both sides realize that [SDI is] a political issue and that grassroots support is important," especially because continued congressional support for Reagan's program hinged on the public's belief in SDI's promise.[6] Beginning in 1983, these two groups and their propaganda campaigns set the tone for future SDI media coverage and provided the public with either visions of promising space technologies or warnings of an unachievable program.

The SDI Announcement

The purpose of Reagan's March 23, 1983, televised address was to explain the administration's continued increases in defense department expenditures. It was a time of prolonged recession, and Americans were concerned with unbalanced budgets from a president who had promised smaller government and economic growth. After providing his rationale for spending increases—the perceived rise of Soviet strength and communist expansionism in Latin America—Reagan next mused on the state of the arms race. He stressed the need for "human spirit" in a nuclear world as well as humanity's desire to rise "above dealing with other nations and human beings by threatening their existence." Reagan believed that Mutually Assured Destruction was "a sad commentary on the human condition." Americans should be capable of "demonstrating peaceful intentions by applying all our abilities and ingenuity to achieving a truly lasting stability." Then, he proposed an alternative to deterrence and the doctrine of MAD:

> Let me share with you a vision of the future which offers hope. It is that we embark on a program to counter the awesome Soviet missile threat with measures that are defensive. Let us turn to the very strengths in technology that spawned our great industrial base and that have given us the quality of life we enjoy today. What if free people could live secure in the knowledge

that their security did not rest upon the threat of instant U.S. retaliation to deter a Soviet attack, that we could intercept and destroy strategic ballistic missiles before they reached our own soil or that of our allies?

While it might be a "formidable, technical task, one that may not be accomplished before the end of this century," Reagan believed that "current technology has attained a level of sophistication where it's reasonable for us to begin this effort." Even if such a program would "take years [and] probably decades of effort on many fronts," was it not "worth every investment necessary to free the world from the threat of nuclear war?" Reagan believed that it was, and he believed that the American people would agree.[7]

Reagan called on "the scientific community in our country, those who gave us nuclear weapons, to turn their great talents now to the cause of mankind and world peace, to give us the means of rendering these nuclear weapons impotent and obsolete." Such rhetoric reflected Reagan's unshakable faith in American ingenuity. If scientists could create an atomic bomb during World War II, then why couldn't they invent some way to save humanity from these very weapons? This idea of technological salvation appealed to Reagan, and his diary entry from that night confirms his optimism: "The big thing today was the 8 P.M. TV speech on all networks about the Nat. Security. . . . I did the speech from the Oval office at 8 & then joined the party for coffee. I guess it was O.K.—they all praised it to the sky & seemed to think it would be a source of debate for some time to come."[8]

Reagan's speech surprised many top-ranking officials, few of whom had little advance knowledge of its final content. Secretary of State George Shultz and Defense Secretary Caspar Weinberger learned of the SDI remarks only hours before Reagan delivered them. Both tried to stop him. Weinberger, then in Lisbon at a NATO conference, called Reagan and urged that all mention of Ballistic Missile Defense (BMD) be dropped from the speech; to a nuclear hawk like Weinberger, SDI could never be as effective as a strong military buildup. Weinberger's top aides, Richard Perle and Ron Lehrman, agreed, and their skepticism made its way to both the *New York Times* and the *Washington Post*. Private, internal White House dissent was becoming public knowledge, and made clear that many in the administration saw SDI as unrealistic. These warnings did little to deter Reagan, who maintained a belief in creating a workable space-based defensive shield.[9]

Where did the president get these futuristic ideas about missile defense? Scholars of SDI cite three likely influences. The first is a 1940 film, *Murder in the Air,* in which Reagan played the role of Brass Bancroft, a special agent tasked with securing the "inertia projector," a top-secret weapon that could fire concentrated energy beams to intercept incoming missiles and provide "the greatest force for world peace ever discovered." Numerous Reagan-era historians have shown the president's tendency to muddle stories with reality, and some credit *Murder in the Air* as the primary inspiration for SDI.[10] Another influence may have been Reagan's desire to dismantle the 1972 Anti-Ballistic Missile (ABM) Treaty, a détente-era agreement that limited superpower production and deployment of ABM systems. On the campaign trail, Reagan had promised to regain Cold War strategic superiority even if it meant renewing America's ABM system.[11] Finally, Martin Anderson, a Reagan aide, cites a 1979 campaign stop at the North American Aerospace Defense Command center as sparking Reagan's interest in SDI. In this narrative, Reagan became dismayed to learn that the United States had no defense against a Soviet first strike, that retaliation was the only option; as president, he began to ponder ways that America could defend itself against nuclear weapons.[12]

Whatever factors shaped Reagan's thinking, by 1983 space-based missile defense programs were hardly new. Since the 1950s, the United States had pursued multiple methods of nuclear defense, primarily anti-satellite weapons and Ballistic Missile Defense systems. Under Eisenhower, the defense department engaged in BMD research programs, such as the Ballistic Missile Boost Intercept program (given the provocative acronym BAMBI). By the 1960s, studies on laser technologies were well under way, and by the Johnson administration the military was engaged in the "Sentinel" program of BMD research. Nixon renamed this BMD program "Safeguard" and narrowed its focus to protect specific US ICBM missile silos. Nixon bargained away Safeguard in the 1972 ABM Treaty, a cornerstone of détente. In short, BMD programs had long been a part of Cold War research and development programs, but historically these programs had been limited in scope or bargained away in superpower negotiations.[13]

Interest in BMD programs resurfaced as the 1970s came to a close, especially after the Soviet invasion of Afghanistan, which prompted hawkish lawmakers to call for new BMD programs. In 1979, Senator Malcolm Wallop (R-WY) submitted an influential report to the conservative defense journal *Strategic Review* which argued for the invention of technologies that might make the threat of ballistic missile attack "obsolete." Wallop's desire to rekindle BMD programs may have been influenced by his state's reliance on pork-barrel military spending programs, or by his young staffer, Angelo Codevilla, a pro–missile defense hawk who rabidly endorsed new space-based defensive systems. Wallop and Codevilla persuaded other senators to join in their BMD crusade, thereby thrusting 1970s-era ground-based ABM system debates into futuristic, space-based BMD proposals of the early 1980s.[14]

In addition to political support, these programs needed scientific support, and no figure was more influential in solidifying Reagan's belief in the possibilities of BMD than Edward Teller, who had stoked Reagan's desire for missile defense as early as 1967. Then the newly elected governor of California, Reagan toured the Lawrence Livermore National Laboratory, where Teller had been researching high-powered X-ray laser beams. There, Teller shared with Reagan his vision of solar- or nuclear-powered lasers that might be positioned on satellites to shoot down incoming ICBMs—a scheme later dubbed "Brilliant Pebbles." The two Californians remained in contact throughout the 1970s; by the 1980s, Teller had become the most notable scientific proponent of SDI, publishing editorials endorsing new technology, expressing optimism about space-based BMD programs, and preaching the possibility of technological missile defense to Congress.[15]

Even more than Wallop, Codevilla, or Teller, the most zealous proponent of BMD was Daniel Graham. A West Point graduate who later served as deputy director of the CIA, Graham was a Reagan military adviser during his 1976 and 1980 campaigns. Easily one of the more hawkish members of Reagan's early coterie, Graham shared his vision of a reinvigorated space race in *Shall America Be Defended?*, a 1979 book arguing that for America to stand strong against the growing Soviet threat, it needed to reassert its military dominance with a workable BMD system. Graham discussed this vision with Reagan in February 1980, arguing that the great military transformations of history, such as evolutions in sea power and air power, meant that the nuclear space race was inevitable. Therefore, it was imperative that the United States take the lead in this next step of military evolution. Graham made similar claims in *Strategic Review*, where he argued that MAD was an outdated strategy that needed to be replaced by the "new strategic framework" of BMD. Such remarks must have appealed to Reagan, as they sound very much like the president's March 23, 1983, pronouncement.[16]

After Reagan assumed the presidency, Graham recognized a chance to make his vision of BDM a reality. He sought support from top administration officials, especially Reagan's then-secretary of state Alexander Haig (Shultz assumed the office in July 1982). Haig, a former Nixon appointee who believed that the best nuclear defense was a strong deterrent, was unreceptive to Graham's proposal. Graham finally found a sympathetic supporter in Karl R. Bendetsen, a conservative businessman with Washington connections. Together, they founded High Frontier, a pro-military NGO with the goal of ensuring US dominance in the Cold War military space race. They received financial support from numerous outside sources, such as the Heritage Foundation and Joseph Coors, the conservative beer magnate. By 1982, High Frontier had raised more than a quarter of a million dollars, which it used to embark on grassroots campaigns that spread pro-BMD propaganda in forty states. High Frontier was gaining notoriety. Encouraged, Graham set out to visit the White House and pitch ideas to his old boss. Reagan liked what he heard, and the reality that Graham's proposed technologies did not yet exist made little difference to the president. Always the optimist, Reagan believed in the ability of American ingenuity and the promise of BMD.[17]

Reagan may have shared Graham's enthusiasm, but numerous cabinet members remained skeptical. In November 1982, Weinberger wrote a stern letter to Graham explaining that whatever the president's personal support was, the White House was "unwilling to commit this nation to a course which calls for . . . a capability that does not currently exist." Weinberger was hardly alone in his pessimism. Robert McFarlane later admitted that he never believed that SDI was valuable except as a bargaining chip at the negotiating table, while George Keyworth was equally doubtful that Graham's vision could be achieved—especially calls for "solar-powered satellites" and "kinetic energy" weapons. This was the early 1980s, and such technologies were a long way off. Keyworth even warned Congress that both the United States and the Soviets were "a great distance away from being able to deploy a large high-energy laser system . . . capable of achieving an ABM objective." These critiques infuriated BMD zealots like Wallop, who demanded that Reagan replace Keyworth; but these debates had little impact on the president, who simply chose to limit SDI discussions to a select group of optimists, including Ed Meese and Richard Allen.[18]

Keyworth's skepticism is notable. As National Science Advisor, he understood that what Graham was asking for was technologically decades away. Also, he knew Graham's reputation, one marred for holding positions and defending them "relentlessly . . . often in the face of the facts." The general's comments—such as his endorsement of allocating defense department research funds to explore extrasensory perception and mental telepathy—had at times alarmed his contemporaries.[19] High Frontier's staff was another cause for concern. Most lacked scientific credentials, and Graham employed a science-fiction writer as a consultant, which may help to explain High Frontier's proposals for manned mini-spacecraft, "kinetic energy" vehicles, and atomic lasers. This sci-fi vision led the defense department to remark that in selling Graham's proposals, High Frontier designer Fred W. Redding Jr. was "not averse to stretching the truth well beyond the breaking point." The administration quickly saw High Frontier as ill-suited to promote or to research BMD programs; Teller's Lawrence Livermore Laboratory was a far more reputable option. That meant cutting off Graham's personal meetings with Reagan, which administration officials saw as an attempt to make an "end run around the bureaucracy." Soon, concerned cabinet members were insulating Reagan from Graham.[20] After the SDI announcement, however, it was too late; the administration had to scramble and put a positive spin on their boss's promise, while Graham, who seems to have successfully influenced the president, turned his attention to convincing the public.

High Frontier

Graham was elated at Reagan's speech, but he was less enthusiastic about the name "Strategic Defense Initiative." Since 1979, Graham had been promoting a program called "High Frontier." What's more, critics quickly adopted the moniker "Star Wars," a pejorative title that connected Reagan's vision to the 1977 lasers-in-space film it seemed to mimic. When the media latched onto the "Star Wars" label, Graham fought back, as did George Lucas, who sued to have his film's title removed from all SDI affiliations. A federal court judge ruled the title in the public domain, however, and the sobriquet stuck.[21] The use of "Strategic Defense Initiative," "Star Wars," or "High Frontier" is revealing, as the choice of term connotes an organization or expert's beliefs about the plausibility of space-based BMD: radical proponents used "High Frontier," moderates preferred "SDI," and skeptics clung to "Star Wars."[22]

The year Reagan unveiled his vision of SDI, Graham released two books promoting the promise of BMD. The first, *A Defense That Defends: Blocking Nuclear Attack*, proposed that nuclear strategy had to develop beyond MAD and toward a "true defense" in space. The second, *High Frontier: A Strategy for National Survival*, provided a detailed "overview of the High Frontier system," which included a "manned space station in low Earth orbit" and some "high-capacity energy systems in space." Moreover, Graham asserted, this system was not far off and might be realized "with technology already in hand and off-the-shelf hardware. None of these requirements demand technological breakthroughs or any commitment to mere scientific theories." Graham applauded President Reagan for having "the courage to start this nation on a road to a true defense." Such praise concerned the White House, as did Graham's inclusion of extended transcriptions from Reagan's March 23, 1983, remarks, both of which gave *High Frontier* the illusion of having an official White House endorsement.[23]

High Frontier's pro-SDI publicity efforts intensified in the days leading up to the broadcast of *The Day After.* Anticipating record ratings for the film, Graham solicited White House support for his "Two Day Media Blitz," which would promote SDI in newspapers and on network television. Graham requested that White House staffers make calls on behalf of High Frontier, especially to conservative philanthropists and potential donors—and solicit $500,000 from each. Not surprisingly, the White House declined to act as Graham's personal phone bank, and Counsel to the President Fred Fielding cautioned others in the administration not to become involved with Graham.[24]

What especially irked Fielding was Graham's repeated use of the president's personal correspondence and public speeches. High Frontier mailers reprinted Reagan's June 3, 1983, letter to Graham, in which the president expressed his appreciation of "the important work that you and your colleagues have done to prepare the way for a more secure America." Reagan also offered that "it was very kind of you to dedicate your book to me."[25] He was referring to Graham's paperback *We Must Defend America and Put an End to MADness,* which not only reprinted part of Reagan's SDI announcement but also included a photograph of Graham and Reagan together in the Oval Office. Finally, on February 22, 1984, Fielding warned Graham that "the President adheres to a policy of generally not endorsing particular fundraising projects, no matter how laudable the objectives of the organizations benefiting from the fundraising," and that "the inclusion of the President's letter in the solicitation for High Frontier . . . is likely to be construed by recipients as an endorsement of the fundraising," a clear violation of White House policy.[26]

The warning didn't phase Graham, who continued to imply close White House cooperation. He did so in one of the most curious pieces of SDI propaganda ever created: High Frontier's "Star Spangled Sweepstakes." In the 1980s, mail-in sweepstakes were common, the most famous being Publishers Clearing House, which featured *Star Search* host and *Tonight Show* cohost Ed McMahon and advertised the possibility of winning millions. Graham modeled his sweepstakes after Publishers Clearing House, except that his mailer pushed a pro-SDI agenda. In it, Graham asked Americans to "enter the All New Star Spangled Sweepstakes . . . for a Safe, Secure America." If they did, they had "over 135 chances to win valuable prizes . . . including a set of U.S. Gold Coins" and an "Early Entry Bonus Prize" of "Big Cash." Three Grand Prizes included $5,000 in gold coins, a Mercury Lynx Hatchback, and an RCA Home Entertainment Center featuring a Colortrak 2000 Projection TV, Selectravision Color Video Camera, and a cassette recorder. Participants might also win a Polaroid Autofocus 600 Instant Camera, a General Electric "Versatron" Countertop Oven, a Regal "Griller" Smokeless Indoor Grill, a Deluxe Re-Dial Telephone, or a Regal "Polly-Pop" Corn Popper . . . all in the name of promoting SDI. Entry into Graham's sweepstakes came with a catch: to win prizes, participants had fill out and return "a questionnaire that will get your feelings about a major national issue counted in the U.S. Congress!: President Reagan's plan to put a network of special satellites in space that would make all of us safe from nuclear missile attack!" In addition to winning prizes, the sweepstakes offered an opportunity for "concerned citizens [to] tell every U.S. senator and congressman what Americans like you really think about this revolutionary approach to ending the 'balance of nuclear terror.'" Graham was "strongly in favor of it . . . after all, everyone enjoys a sweepstakes. It's an ideal way to reach great numbers of Americans with the facts about this plan to free mankind from the menace of nuclear confrontation."[27]

Graham's mailer also included a not-so-subtle dig at the nuclear freeze campaign and continued to imply White House support. "Seven out of ten Democrats said that they wanted [an SDI] system. So you see, it's not a matter of politics [and if] High Frontier had its way, ALL nuclear missiles would soon become unusable antiques! Frankly, I think that's a far better idea than even a nuclear freeze. After all, a nuclear freeze . . . would still leave the world threatened by arsenals of nuclear missiles." Graham also promised that "the proposed new space-based shield against nuclear weapons could actually save tax dollars [because] the technology needed for [SDI] either already exists or has been well proven . . . once it's working it will replace [other] far costlier military hardware." In August 1985, a confused citizen forwarded the "Star Spangled Sweepstakes" to the White House along with a letter asking if Reagan had endorsed the mailing. The letter never made it to the president's desk, but Counsel to the President Fred Fielding asked leadership at the Republican National Committee if they knew of Graham's most recent efforts. The RNC responded that they did not, leaving Fielding to draft a response simply stating that "the President has not endorsed the sweepstakes nor is he in any way involved with its operation" and that Graham's sweepstakes was "entirely a private effort."[28]

In another private effort that made unrealistic promises about SDI, in 1984 High Frontier produced *A Defense That Defends*. The film featured Lorne Greene, a Canadian actor best known for his role as Ben Cartwright in the television Western *Bonanza* and as Commander Adama in the sci-fi series *Battlestar Gallactica*. *A Defense That Defends* opens with a cardigan-clad Greene walking through a garden and sharing his thoughts about SDI:

> I'd like to talk to you about a very important idea: a non-nuclear defense against nuclear missiles. If you've heard it called "Star Wars" that's unfortunate, because it's a misleading name for the concept. It conjures up notions of futuristic science fiction space machines blasting away at each other in outer space. I'm not a scientist—although I wish I were sometimes—but I do know the difference between fantasy and reality . . . after all I did command a fantasy spaceship, as some of you may recall. Now the proper name for the idea I mentioned is "High Frontier," not "Star Wars." It's a proposal for a non-threatening, non-nuclear defense system to be set up in the high frontier of space to defend against the most awesome of destructive weapons: the nuclear ballistic missile. The concept was put forward in a report prepared by a group of non-governmental scientists and engineers as a result of an effort called "High Frontier." The report was the catalyst behind the President's launching of his Strategic Defense Initiative in March of 1983.

Next, Greene pondered, "What would happen if only a few nuclear missiles were launched at us, by accident, by a breakdown in communications, or even on purpose?" The reality was that the president could do little to defend America, at least not "until High Frontier is set into place." What followed were graphics depicting a workable program consisting of a "three-tiered" system that included ground-based ABM guns, satellite-mounted space lasers, and a high-tech computer infrastructure connecting it all. Greene concludes the documentary by promising nuclear abolition, for High Frontier "so effectively reduces the risks of a Soviet first strike, [America] will have little need to continue amassing ever-larger arsenals of nuclear weapons." If the United States only "put the same effort into High Frontier as we did putting a man on the moon," the system could be "operational by the end of the decade. This is no fantasy," assured Greene, but Americans needed to act fast, as the "Soviets were already at work" on their own program and had "sent seven space stations into orbit" from a secret camp known as "Star Town," where Communist cosmonauts were trained to man these satellites for up to two hundred consecutive days. The Soviet commitment, therefore, was "clear, constant, and determined." America's choice should be equally clear.[29]

At this point, perhaps consumed with its reelection campaign or devoted to new diplomatic efforts with the Soviet Union, the White House paid little attention to High Frontier's film—but another NGO did. Alarmed at the false promises made by Graham and his organization, and convinced that no such system could ever work, the UCS responded with their own anti–Star Wars propaganda. In combating pro-SDI propaganda, the UCS's methods were strikingly similar to High Frontier's: both groups courted White House recognition and support; both began their publicity campaigns with literature and later transitioned into television documentaries; and both sought, and gained, celebrity endorsements. With similar tactics but a different message, the UCS engaged High Frontier in what would be an ongoing media war.

The Union of Concerned Scientists Respond

From the start, numerous antinuclear advocacy groups opposed Star Wars, including the Physicians for Social Responsibility and the Committee for a Sane Nuclear Policy. Both feared that missile defense would destabilize deterrence, or worse, through human or computer error, trigger an accidental nuclear war. Yet no group opposed SDI more persistently or publicly than the Union of Concerned Scientists. Founded in 1969 in Cambridge, Massachusetts, the UCS engaged in "research, public advocacy, and education activities" to inform Americans about issues of "nuclear arms control, energy policy, and nuclear-power safety." The group gained media attention due to its notable membership, such as the antinuclear activist and Nobel Prize–winning physicist Hans Bethe. After Nixon signed the 1972 ABM Treaty, the UCS shifted its focus toward containing nuclear power; but in 1981, after Reagan assumed the presidency and administration officials began talking tough about winning a nuclear war, the UCS returned to the disarmament cause.[30]

The UCS made clear its hopes to "Ban Space Weapons" even before the SDI announcement. In February 1983, they publicized a petition that included signatures from former Manhattan Project member Victor Weisskopf, former Nixon administration NSA director Noel Gayler, Cornell University physics professor and Nobel laureate Hans Bethe, and Columbia University professor and Nobel Prize winner Isidor I. Rabi. The petition's high-profile signatures signaled that experts in physics and defense did not side with

BMD programs. Printed in the *New York Times* and later published in the *Bulletin of the Atomic Scientists,* it urged to both the Soviet Union and the United States that any "testing or deployment of any weapons in space . . . significantly increases the likelihood of warfare on Earth."[31]

That was February 1983; Reagan's SDI announcement one month later solidified the organization's resolve, and especially Sagan's. The Cornell professor and celebrity scientist first learned about Star Wars from a hospital bed, where he lay recovering from a botched surgical procedure. Both Sagan and his wife, Ann Druyan, saw SDI as a quixotic program, one that could be easily overwhelmed with enough decoy missiles. Sagan also recognized flaws in Reagan's logic about a defensive shield; logically, SDI would only prompt the Soviets to intensify their nuclear buildup and fuel the arms race. Sagan immediately dictated to Druyan an anti-SDI petition replete with the names of prominent friends, including astronaut turned senator John Glenn and Japanese prime minister Yasuhiro Nakasone. After four frantic nights of making phone calls, Druyan attained hundreds of signatures. After leaving the hospital, Sagan announced to colleagues that he was abandoning his role in NASA's *Galileo* space project to devote his "energies [to] saving the world from nuclear holocaust."[32]

In this crusade, Sagan wasted little time. On March 27, less than a week after Reagan's SDI announcement, he and the physicist Richard L. Garwin republished a UCS petition to ban weapons in space. Appearing in the *New York Times,* it called for "the United States, the Soviet Union and other space-faring nations . . . [to] negotiate, for their benefit and for the benefit of the human species, a treaty to ban weapons of any kind from space, and to prohibit damage to or destruction of satellites of any nation."[33] Next, the UCS released "Anti-Satellite Weapons: Arms Control or Arms Race?," a report that emphasized America's need to maintain a stable deterrent as well as renew the 1972 ABM Treaty. Kendall forwarded a copy of this report to Reagan, but likely the report never made it to his desk. Instead, the State Department drafted a terse response explaining that while the White House took UCS concerns about nuclear weapons seriously, ending SDI research would "allow the Soviets to retain their operational anti-satellite system while prohibiting us from developing and deploying one of our own." Additionally, the UCS's accusation that the Soviets might "lose confidence in their [missile defense] system" was "rather speculative." Apparently, the administration was shielding Reagan not only from pro-SDI zealotry of High Frontier but also from criticism by the scientific community.[34]

In June the UCS published a teaching module for American schools. Titled *Choices: A Unit on Conflict and Nuclear War,* it provided "ten lessons on the evolution of the nuclear arms race, the nature and consequences of using nuclear weapons, and new ways that conflicts among nations might be resolved." Aimed at "junior high school level" students, *Choices* warned about the steady growth of the global nuclear arsenal, recommended that students read antinuclear literature such as *The Fate of the Earth,* and emphasized the need for superpower cooperation. Reagan angrily denounced *Choices* as a "brainwashing" project "aimed at frightening" school children.[35] Perturbed, on June 6, Kendall sent another letter to the White House, this time accusing Reagan of suppressing "free discussion of the issues of war and peace in the nation's schools" and criticizing the administration's attempts at censorship. To Kendall, "what has scared our nation's children is talk of waging and winning nuclear war." Also, he hoped that the administration was "not trying to intimidate American educators into silence on this issue." *Choices* clearly had increased animosity between the UCS and the White House, and future anti–Star Wars publications would only fuel that acrimony.[36]

By 1984, the public attacks on SDI had intensified. Vintage published a "special edition" paperback, *The Fallacy of Star Wars,* which was based on studies conducted by the UCS. The book provided a detailed case against SDI, as did an op-ed piece carried by United Press International and published in the *Los Angeles Times* in which Kendall called Star Wars "naïve." Scientists, Kendall boasted, know very well that "there is not a shred of scientific evidence that it can be effective."[37] It would only take a few submarine-launched ballistic missiles to fly under SDI, or some ICBM decoys, to confuse or overwhelm any SDI program. In response to these comments, the administration restricted Kendall's access to the White House, which led the UCS to replace him with a new spokesperson, Jonathan Dean. A former arms control adviser and US ambassador, Dean sought to move "the organization towards a more constructive approach" with the White House and immediately requested a meeting with National Security Advisor Robert McFarlane. He hoped to discuss "an agreement to limit anti-satellite weapons; a linking of talks on offensive weapons with negotiation on defensive weapons; steps to reduce the risk of conventional and nuclear war in Europe; [and] a long-term and practical plan to sharply reduce the now large inventories of nuclear weapons."[38] That was January 4, 1985; one month later, NSC staffer Sven Kraemer had to politely ask McFarlane to respond to Dean's request. McFarlane acquiesced, but only "grudgingly." The national security adviser wasn't the only one annoyed with the UCS. In a June 27, 1985, response to a letter from Princeton professor Eugene Wigner, President Reagan was candid: "May I say, I've been concerned for some time by the actions and statements of that organization [the UCS] which seems to depart now and then from the truth in pleading its cause."[39]

Still, Dean met with McFarlane, and while it may have been painful for the national security adviser to entertain the UCS's disarmament views, private meetings had their advantages. White House memoranda show that while UCS "scientists remain highly skeptical about SDI's technical feasibility and its stabilization potential," private consultations were much better than public criticisms. Kraemer advised McFarlane: "[The UCS] think they are being constructive by no longer attacking SDI frontally . . . however, they clearly remain out to block, or crimp, the program severely." McFarlane's meeting allowed the UCS to believe they were being taken seriously, while Kraemer recommended that "after listening to their opening remarks," simply "reaffirm the President's strong interest both in arms reductions and in reshaping strategic deterrence." Put simply, McFarlane hoped private meetings would quell public criticisms.[40]

While Dean wrangled with the administration, Sagan was busy creating an anti-SDI multimedia presentation to use for talks on college campuses and private meetings with political leaders. To create the slideshow presentation *Weapons in Space*, Sagan used his television connections, including his longtime illustrator from *Cosmos*, Jon Lomberg, and the composer Bob Derkach. For narrator, Sagan got a high-profile celebrity endorsement: the instantly recognizable voice of James Earl Jones. It was a fitting choice; not only had Jones appeared in the atomic satire *Dr. Strangelove*, but his deep baritone was the voice of Darth Vader in the original *Star Wars* trilogy.

Weapons in Space opens with images from the *Star Wars* films juxtaposed with drawings of what Reagan's Star Wars program might look like. As the images click past, Jones narrates:

Space weapons, laser battles, and death stars exist only in the movies. I'm James Earl Jones, and I would like to talk to you about this space war fantasy becoming a reality. The greatest fear people have today is that of nuclear war. Recently, space-based defenses against ballistic missiles have been proposed that allegedly would make nuclear weapons impotent and obsolete. The Union of Concerned Scientists, a national organization with extensive experience in weapons technology, has completed a study of the proposed systems. They have found that space defense is a dangerous fantasy. None of the systems have been built. All of them face enormous technical hurdles and staggering costs. Worst of all, none of them will protect us from the huge missile buildup they will provoke.[41]

Jones acknowledged SDI supporters' belief that Reagan's program would "defend our country against intercontinental ballistic missiles," but explained that this was a dangerous dream. The reality was that the Soviets could easily overwhelm any Star Wars system with ICBM decoys, more medium-range missiles, or nuclear "suitcase" bombs. Because the "technical assessment of these weapons is very bleak, their operation under battle conditions will always be in doubt." Instead of SDI, the White House should return to the negotiating table, as "the treaty limiting anti-ballistic missile defenses is the most important existing arms control agreement . . . [but] it will be swept aside if we proceed with space defenses." Jones concluded the presentation with the UCS's clarion call: keep weapons out of space. "America has pioneered the use of space technology. Every day satellites affect and improve our lives. NASA's explorations have brought out the best human qualities of courage, ingenuity, and curiosity; but it is negotiated agreements, the force of reason—not space technology—that will save us from nuclear annihilation." The call to action was clear: the American public needed to "demand that all weapons be banned from space." His multimedia presentation in place, Sagan embarked on a university campus tour to spread the word about the dangers of SDI. He also sought to reach millions of Americans via television, as did High Frontier.

The Great "Star Wars" PR War

Nineteen eighty-four was an election year, and in the run-up to the presidential reelection campaign both organizations created television commercials to publicize their competing visions. In October 1984, High Frontier broadcast the "Crayola" ad. A crayon drawing of stick figures, a square house, and a frowning-face sun, the thirty-second spot featured a child's voiceover: "I asked my daddy what this 'Star Wars' stuff is all about. He said that right now we can't protect from nuclear weapons, and that's why the President wants to build a Peace Shield. It'd stop missiles in outer space . . . so they couldn't hit our house. Then nobody could win a war, and if nobody could win a war, there's no reason to start one. My daddy's smart." Animated crayon-drawn missiles descend, harmlessly popping when they make contact with a bluish arc across the top of the picture. As this "Peace Shield" protects the family, the sun's frowning face transforms into a smile and an American flag flies in front of the house.[42] The use of crayon art to promote a technologically advanced program to protect Americans from thermonuclear war understandably earned High Frontier some criticism. Numerous newspaper editorial cartoons ridiculed the commercial for being overly simplistic.[43]

The Committee for a Strong and Peaceful America—a collation of eight antinuclear groups—lampooned the "Crayola" ad in their "Space Wars I" commercial. In it, a child watches High Frontier's "Crayola" ad on television while playing with letter blocks. The narrator explains that the boy, Matthew, "has the same problem the White House does. He's trying to turn Star Wars into something called the 'Peace Shield.' But it doesn't fit. Because Matthew is learning what adults already know: when someone wants to mislead you, they try to change the name. But when you look closer, it's still the same old thing." As the ad ends, Matthew, after considerable effort, has reconfigured his blocks. Now, instead of "Peace Shield," they read "Space Wars." "Space Wars I" conveyed that Reagan's SDI would not offer a shield but provide a way to weaponize space.[44]

The UCS created its own child-centered response to the High Frontier commercial. In May 1985, networks aired its twenty-second "Twinkle, Twinkle" ad, which showed a pajama-clad boy peering out his bedroom window. Gripping a teddy bear and gazing at the sky, he sings "Twinkle, Twinkle, Little Star" as one star grows increasingly bright and finally explodes. The screen is flooded with a white light while James Earl Jones narrates: "The heavens are for wonder, not for war. Stop Star Wars. Stop weapons in space." The ad was part of the UCS's "new offensive" against SDI, one that aimed to "counter the administration's claims about Star Wars" and compete against High Frontier's pro-SDI commercial. A second ad touted the UCS's scientific expertise, adding an adult tone to a thus-far childish television exchange. It featured Victor Weisskopf, who looked into the camera and expressed his hope for arms control: "I helped design the atomic bomb. I know what would happen in a nuclear war. I only wish President Reagan did."[45]

The networks took notice of this ongoing media war, and on May 30, 1985, *NBC Nightly News* noted that UCS commercials coincided with recent Soviet requests that the United States halt SDI research. CBS gave the organization favorable coverage, informing viewers that fifty-four Nobel Prize–winning scientists and more than half the members of the American Academy of Science had joined the antinuclear cause: "Never before have so many noted scientists opposed [a presidential] administration." CBS also aired Kendall's remarks that SDI would only "reinvigorate an already nasty and very dangerous nuclear arms race."[46] On November 14, 1985, spokespeople from each organization debated SDI on the *CBS Evening News*. In the heated exchange, Kendall attacked High Frontier's "Crayola" ad for being simplistic, calling it a "fraud on the American public." Graham countered that at least in High Frontier's ad the "child gets protected [while] in the Union of Concerned Scientists [commercial], she [*sic*] gets blown up." In a few words, Graham had summarized the level of debate thus far. In reality, there was no SDI system. These ads were simply about pessimism or optimism regarding an unrealized program.[47]

The efforts of High Frontier and the UCS had so successfully shaped public perceptions of SDI that in 1985 these visions were incorporated into two Hollywood films: *Spies Like Us* and *Real Genius*. In *Spies Like Us* two NSA decoys (played by Dan Aykroyd and Chevy Chase) embark on a mission in which they launch a Soviet ICBM at the United States to test an SDI system—a plotline based on the UCS criticism that the only way to test such a system would be with a dangerous nuclear attack. In *Real Genius*, students at an MIT-like university create a high-powered laser beam, only to discover that their professor has sold the prototype to the US government to be mounted as a satellite weapon—a plot very like High Frontier's proposals.[48] These films show the extent to which the UCS and High Frontier, and not the White House, had framed popular ideas about SDI.

In December 1985 the ongoing media battle became the focus of a *Time* magazine article titled "The Great 'Star Wars' P.R. War." It recapped pro- and anti-SDI propaganda and asked Washington public relations experts to weigh in. Experts agreed that High Frontier and UCS, and not the government, had delineated the boundaries of SDI's potential: High Frontier's ads showed that "if you oversimplify Star Wars, it sounds terrific," while UCS ads revealed that the more you "explain [SDI], the worse it sounds." The administration's goal, therefore, would be to pursue a more moderate course and scale back the rhetoric. "The goal is to stay in the middle, not to be like High Frontier, which has been labeled as zealots, or the Union of Concerned Scientists, who have also been labeled as zealots."[49] This was the approach that the Reagan administration pursued through the efforts of its official Strategic Defense Initiative Organization (SDIO).

The SDIO

Created in 1984, the SDIO was an independent body within the Department of Defense devoted solely to SDI research. Its director was the former astronaut Lt. Gen. James A. Abrahamson Jr. Faced with NGOs' SDI propaganda on television, Abrahamson hoped to articulate SDI's real potential to Congress and to the press. In the summer of 1985, the *New York Times* ran a slew of detailed stories on the increasingly public organization, which hoped to move public opinion away from skepticism.[50] "There is very little question that we can build a very highly effective defense against ballistic missiles someday," Abrahamson stated. Promising that it was only a matter of time before Reagan's dream became a reality, however, became problematic into Reagan's second term.[51]

To sway the public, the NSC devised a strategy: the SDIO would enlist "pro-SDI scientists," especially "older, sage types," to lead "collateral press opportunities" that might deflect UCS critiques. In this public relations campaign, nostalgia was key, and the SDIO should emphasize that "SDI is the scientific challenge [of] this generation, as Apollo was to scientists of the '60s." These types of positive statements had "excellent regional press possibilities." Overall, SDIO-affiliated scientists were to stress that "SDI research has made remarkable progress." Repetition was critical: "If we say this long enough, with conviction, then public impression will turn to the assurity [*sic*] that SDI is technically feasible."[52]

Convincing the public that SDI was within reach would "help with two constant struggles." First, it addressed the concerns of the Congressional Budget Office. During Reagan's second term, Congress called for a "return on investment" for SDI. Initially, the Department of Defense had allotted $1.4 billion to the SDIO, so Abrahamson's promise of a "return on investment" was imperative. Congressional leaders had begun questioning the value of SDI funding, especially the fiscally conservative Democratic senator William Proxmire. On CBS's *Face the Nation,* Proxmire called the case against Star Wars "overwhelming."[53] The pressure mounting, by 1986 the SDIO began its "new program" in the hopes of validating its spending for congressional skeptics. If the organization obtained "strong Congressional endorsement" it might achieve "new funding and [remove] restrictive amendments to research and development and production cooperation." The SDIO now sought to "foster Allied participation and support for SDI and gain strong Congressional endorsement." Doing so would provide "a real justification for increased funding for [Fiscal Year] 1986." Congressional endorsements might also "take pressure off the overall SDI budgetary squeeze [and] provide SDI research . . . with an outlet for a tangible product." If the SDIO could turn research and development efforts into tangible defense innovations, it might maintain congressional funding.[54]

The SDIO's second goal was to present SDI as a program making steady progress. For years, the UCS had made accusations that Reagan was "negotiating away arms reductions for a pie in the ski [sic] idea." In response, the SDIO bombarded the American public with reports of technological advances, and it mattered little how minor the development or breakthrough.[55] Abrahamson believed that for too long "Hill critics" had been criticizing "the program for its lack of organization and clear objectives," so the SDIO "should respond by specifying what military missions SDI must accomplish in addition and prior to deployment of 'thoroughly effective' defenses." Translation: Forget foolproof missile defense; instead, sell SDI as a program to enhance "protection of our allies and troops . . . against tactical ballistic missiles," safeguard "our key satellites against attack," and "contribute to theatre and conventional force improvements." This shift was significant. The SDIO had rejected Reagan's promise to make nuclear weapons "impotent and obsolete"; now, Abrahamson would sell SDI as another deterrence or tactical-level defense enhancer.[56]

Abrahamson's new strategy relied on heavy press coverage. Beginning in 1986, a number of network news programs ran pieces on SDI's technological "breakthroughs." One story showed ecstatic scientists raising champagne toasts at the progress of their "railgun" prototype, a cannon that shot projectiles with enough force to pierce the metal of a hypothetical incoming missile. The railgun fit perfectly into Abrahamson's strategy: it avoided unrealistic promises and instead promoted incremental progress toward a workable missile defense. Of course, the railgun was not in space, and the metal it pierced was not even in motion let alone hurtling through the atmosphere. A far cry from High Frontier's visions of X-ray lasers, but any successful test—no matter how rudimentary—meant good publicity.[57]

It did not take long for the UCS to ascertain Abrahamson's strategy. In 1986 the organization responded with the paperback *Empty Promise: The Growing Case against Star Wars* and a companion piece, *False Frontier,* an hour-long video documentary criticizing SDI. Both stressed that Reagan's "peace shield" was an impossibility; even in a "best case" scenario, SDI "would always act like a sieve" letting numerous nuclear missiles through. "One of the ironies of the SDI debate," the UCS bemoaned, "is that the critics are gradually being proved correct, while the program itself continues to receive ample appropriations from Congress." These continued appropriations resulted from Abrahamson's strategy. When the SDIO shifted away from promoting a "Peace Shield" toward a "new purpose [of] enhanced deterrence," it allowed Congress to validate expenditures and continue funneling Defense money into their districts. The UCS noted this "complete change in the goal of the Star Wars program. No longer do we hear President Reagan's promise that the SDI will render 'nuclear weapons impotent and obsolete'; to the contrary, it now appears that the SDI will ultimately be designed to protect nuclear weapons, not our people."[58] The UCS pinpointed Abrahamson's strategy but could do little to halt congressional appropriations for SDI.

By 1987 the SDIO had begun working with an established pro-defense organization, the American Defense Preparedness Association (ADPA). High Frontier had been producing pro-SDI books, pamphlets, commercials, and documentaries for years, but they received little White House support. Reagan administration officials were far more comfortable with the established ADPA than Graham's fringe group. Founded in 1919, the ADPA promoted itself as "the only organization in the U.S. which unites, through membership and activities, military officers and civilian defense officials; key executives and managers in military installations, plants, and factories; scientists and engineers; weapons designers . . . and other concerned American citizens." This "nationwide society" was an "educational . . . nonpolitical and nonprofit organization [that] promoted national defense." By the 1980s, the organization had over forty thousand members and published a national security newsletter, *The Common Defense.* The ADPA, then, was a long-established pro-military organization that had clout within defense and policy circles.[59]

The ADPA now engaged in its own SDI publicity campaign. Like High Frontier, the ADPA battled the UCS, but unlike Graham's organization—and in keeping with Abrahamson's strategy—the organization only promoted available technologies that could enhance deterrence. The ADPA president, retired general Henry Miley, focused his energies not on television ads or nightly news broadcasts but within Washington. A Beltway insider, Miley knew established defense industry members: Paul Nitze of the Committee on the Present Danger frequently gave talks on SDI to the ADPA; the ADPA's 1987 "industry award" went to Defense Secretary Weinberger; President Reagan recorded videotaped remarks for the organization which applauded the "substantial progress" and "great promise" of SDI research. The ADPA, therefore, was a respected national security organization with close ties to administration officials.[60]

In 1987 the ADPA worked within the White House to produce an SDI documentary that could "present a variety of major viewpoints on SDI and related strategic issues." They enlisted Abrahamson, Shultz, Weinberger, and Reagan's most recent national security adviser, Frank C. Carlucci, to appear in it. (Graham, who had been directed repeatedly to refrain from including administration endorsement, would have been infuriated to learn that ADPA camera crews had gained such access.) The participants were provided questions together with "proposed response" bullet points in advance of the filming. These talking points avoided any mention of a "Peace Shield," and instead touted the incremental progress being made toward enhancing deterrence. For example, the ADPA asked Carlucci to promote SDI research as "vital to future Western security" interests and to say that SDI would help the United States "keep the peace" and "maintain a strategic balance." None of this rhetoric transcended MAD or stuck to Reagan's call to render nuclear weapons "impotent and obsolete."[61]

With these efforts, the SDIO rescinded Reagan's original stated intention for SDI, repeatedly maintaining that SDI had never been an attempt to engage in a new, imaginative program of space-based BMD, but rather that Reagan had simply responded to "deep Soviet involvement in strategic defense." In fact, the Soviets had been the first to initiate SDI-like programs, and these programs required "the West to have its own defensive options ASAP." The ADPA also maintained that the Soviets "have been deeply involved in strategic defense programs . . . for at least 15–20 years" and that already "their laser weapon program alone involves some 10,000 highly trained scientists and engineers and costs the U.S. equivalent of about $1 [billion] a year. [US] deterrence would be severely undermined if the Soviets had both their first strike–orientated offense and a defense which could take away the credibility of our threat to retaliate." America's SDI program only reinforced long-standing "NATO strategy . . . to deter any Soviet aggression, nuclear or conventional." Before SDI, the Soviets enjoyed a "virtual monopoly in strategic defense." With SDI that monopoly has "now ended . . . and that's a good thing."[62]

The ADPA documentary also addressed UCS criticism. The prepared talking points emphasized that Reagan had never believed in a "leakproof" defense, just improved deterrence. Carlucci certainly did "not believe the

President had promised too much of SDI," and besides, SDI did not need to be perfect to be effective. According to Carlucci, "if we can establish effective defenses [or] the effectiveness of deterrence thru defense" SDI would act as "a level for deep reductions in offensive arsenals." Any accusations that Reagan had no "clear goal or mission for SDI" were unfounded. SDI was always about enhancing deterrence.[63]

Finished in 1987, *SDI: A Prospect for Peace,* was a film production of Smith & Harroff. The final bill was $250,000. Carlucci appears in it, as does Weinberger and Indiana senator Dan Quayle. To add scientific credibility, the film also features interviews with John Pike of the Federation of American Scientists. *SDI: A Prospect for Peace* was never broadcast nationally, and likely the SDIO never intended for the general public ever to see it. Instead, White House aides and congressional leaders attended a private screening of the film at Washington's L'Enfant Plaza Hotel. Director of Presidential Appointments and Scheduling Frederick Ryan asked if Reagan could "plug" the film, so the president previewed it at Camp David and was later "very enthusiastic" about taping a promotional video. But few would see Reagan's remarks, as they were aimed at Washington insiders and members of Congress.[64]

SDI: A Prospect for Peace's very limited viewership exemplified the SDIO's shift in strategy: minimize discussing expenditures in public and maximize efforts to quietly maintain funding for the program. This film was propaganda aimed at congressional leaders who approved budgets, and it showed that SDI was making tangible, steady progress that would provide a return on investment. If budgets are any indicator, the ADPA's film worked. SDI funding increased from roughly $3 billion by 1986 to more than $4 billion by 1987. According to some analyses, by the end of the Reagan presidency total SDI-related funding topped $22 billion.[65]

This was a curious media battle over a still-fictional vision of missile defense. As Edward Linenthal assessed, "There has never been a *nonexistent* weapons system that has generated more passionate veneration and contempt" than SDI.[66] The propaganda examined in this chapter constitutes only part of a much larger puzzle—SDI played a role in political, military, and economic issues of the Reagan presidency. Nevertheless, an examination of this evolution of SDI propaganda shows, again, that during the early 1980s American mass media became a contested forum in which arms race proponents and cultural activists battled over public opinion. Reagan may have introduced SDI, but it was two NGOs, who made use of print media, multimedia presentations, television ads, and even a mail-in sweepstakes, who defined public perceptions of the program.

What allowed for these NGOs to have such an influence came down to the fact that, put simply, "Star Wars" did not exist. As Linenthal observed, Americans "easily forget . . . that there is no 'it'; there is only the 'I' in SDI." Reagan's initiative, depending on the interpretation, had provided either "an *appealing* vision of a world made secure through missile defense or an *appalling* vision of a world nearer nuclear catastrophe because of missile defense." These were the opposing sides that High Frontier and the UCS assumed, and neither organization's extreme vision was politically preferable for the White House. The "Star Wars PR War" taught Washington insiders, and the White House, that future SDI propaganda needed to focus on short-term, tangible goals to maintain funding.[67] In scaling back SDI's promise, the SDIO ensured continued congressional funding. The lesson was simple: sometimes the most profitable approach was to avoid public discussions altogether.

Conclusion

In 1984, Random House released the latest book by Theodore Geisel, better known as Dr. Seuss. *The Butter Battle Book* was the story of the Yooks and the Zooks, two tribes warring over an ideological difference: the Yooks ate their toast butter side up, the Zooks, butter side down. To defend their beliefs, they engage in a dangerously escalating arms race; by the end of the story, both had developed "Big-Boy Bameroos," tiny but deadly weapons of mass destruction that could wipe out civilization entirely. Geisel left the story unresolved, with the Yooks and the Zooks in a tense standoff. It was a timely metaphor for the events of the past three years, a period in which the Cold War arms race predominated American politics and the fear of nuclear war permeated American culture.

President Reagan had his own metaphor for the nuclear standoff: two cowboys with cocked pistols pointed at each other's head, and neither cowboy dared to relinquish his weapon. It was a metaphor that, in 1982, fit the Reagan administration's worldview.[1] Largely composed of hardline anticommunists pulled from Team B and the Committee on the Present Danger, these men saw the Cold War as a Manichaean struggle that pitted good Americans against evil totalitarian communists. Administration officials such as Richard Pipes, Caspar Weinberger, and T. K. Jones had talked boastfully of winning a nuclear war, and their remarks contributed to the rise of antinuclear activism. For much of 1982, the Reagan administration had to respond with public pronouncements about considering a freeze or bilateral treaties with the Soviets, but the archives reveal that these amounted to little more than propaganda.

By 1983, however, that attitude began to change. Pragmatic administration officials, those willing to negotiate with the Soviets, were replacing the hard-liners. The most important figure in this shift was George Shultz, who had replaced Alexander Haig as secretary of state in 1982. In addition, the June 1983 appointment of Jack Matlock as head of the NSC further led the White House down the path of pragmatism. William Clark resigned in October 1982; Pipes had left just ten months previous; and while Weinberger stayed on, Shultz had gained the all-important support of Nancy Reagan, which helped earn him the president's favor over the defense secretary. "In 1981 and 1982, the most hawkish position tended to win out," James Graham Wilson has noted of the Reagan administration, but by late 1983 that was changing. "Unlike the hardliners William Casey, William Clark, Richard Pipes, Jeane Kirkpatrick, and Caspar Weinberger, Shultz and Matlock believed that the Soviet Union possessed the capacity to reform."[2]

In time, so did Reagan, especially after learning that in November 1983 a NATO war game, "Able Archer 83," almost triggered a nuclear war. How could a common Cold War exercise almost lead to nuclear annihilation? Shortly after Reagan's 1980 presidential campaign—one laden with hardline rhetoric—Soviet leader Yuri Andropov tasked the KGB with investigating a possible US first strike. Superpower relations deteriorated over the next few years, and by the end of 1983 tensions had reached a new high. It was a year in which Reagan called the Soviet Union "the focus of evil" in the modern world and the Soviets were internationally condemned for the KAL 007 incident; additionally, the Kremlin remained concerned over SDI as well as the arrival of US Euromissiles. So, when NATO engaged the war game, the KGB took to high alert. According to the historian Christopher Andrews, the KGB saw the exercise as a possible "beginning of the countdown towards a nuclear first strike." Reagan was shocked to learn that the Soviets feared that America would fire first. "I feel the Soviets are . . . so paranoid about being attacked that . . . we ought to tell them no one here has any intention of doing anything like that."[3] At face value, this statement means Reagan failed to recognize the impact that years of bellicose language—much of it his own—had on super-power relations. It took months of overt gestures, and more pragmatism, to assure the Soviets of America's willingness to negotiate.

In this shift toward pragmatism, Shultz was the indispensable man. By 1983, the secretary of state had opened lines of communication with the Soviet statesman Anatoly Dobrynin; by 1984, Reagan was in talks with their long-standing diplomat Andrei Gromyko, and in 1985, after the death of Konstantin Chernenko, Reagan found a Soviet leader he could work with:

Mikhail Gorbachev. As he embarked on a second term, many conservatives balked at Reagan's growing political relationship with the new Soviet premier, but Reagan remained engaged. Clearly, the climate had changed since 1982.[4] After two highly publicized but largely unsuccessful superpower summits, in 1987 Reagan and Gorbachev agreed on an arms reduction treaty, the Intermediate-Range Nuclear Forces (INF) Treaty, which removed the threat of IRBMs from the European theater. The Euromissiles were gone, global nuclear fear abated, and although antinuclear activism didn't disappear, it did diminish considerably.[5]

Despite being a highly consequential president, Reagan has remained conspicuously absent throughout this book, but not without reason. Notorious for delegating duties, Reagan largely left it to administration officials to defend his policies; much of this book has focused on their efforts. But perhaps antinuclear cultural activism succeeded in reaching Reagan directly. Consider *The Day After*. Reagan had screened an advance copy of the film on October 10, 1983; that night, his diary entry reads: "I ran the tape of the movie ABC is running Nov. 20. It's called *The Day After* in which Lawrence is wiped out in a nuclear war with Russia. It is powerfully done, all $7 million worth. It's very effective and left me greatly depressed. [My] own reaction was one of our having to do all we can to have a deterrent and to see there is never a nuclear war." Shortly after viewing *The Day After,* Reagan participated in a briefing on US plans for nuclear war that "in several ways . . . paralleled those in the ABC movie." Disturbingly for Reagan, "there were still some people in the Pentagon who claimed a nuclear war was 'winnable.' I thought they were crazy."[6]

Did *The Day After* drive home the horrors of nuclear war in ways military briefings or memoranda could not? It's impossible to gauge the impact of one film, but this entry remains a rare, direct quote regarding nuclear weapons from an often inscrutable president. Many biographers and historians have recounted how Reagan, a former actor, maintained a love of films that never diminished. Astute cabinet members recognized this and adapted to Reagan's learning style; the CIA even began creating short films to brief Reagan on world leaders and recent geopolitical developments.[7] The power of film may even have led Reagan to implement the first cyber security National Security Decision Directive (NSDD-145), a measure inspired after he watched the 1983 film *Wargames*.[8] For Reagan, movies mattered. This mention of *The Day After* in his diary shows that antinuclear cultural activism drove home the horrors of nuclear war to the president in ways that grassroots demonstrations could not.

Scholars will continue to debate which historical actors or factors deserve primary credit for ending the Cold War. Some see Gorbachev as the most important figure; others give credit to Reagan. There are camps that variously see economic differences, grassroots protests, human rights, the pressures of globalization, and continued scientific activism as important contributors to the end of the Cold War. But battles over public opinion, those waged between the Reagan administration and antinuclear cultural activists, deserve to be included in that list of factors. Whether or not Reagan had a genuine "reversal" in his feelings toward the Soviets remains debatable; more certain is that throughout Reagan's first term, the onslaught of antinuclear media prompted the administration to act; perhaps more important, it provided opportunities for the White House to promote a new approach to superpower relations. As that pivot took place, the public consumed this new rhetoric of preventing a nuclear war; by the 1987 landmark INF Treaty, what began as "a propaganda exercise" proved genuine. As Reagan's second term came to a close, Gorbachev continued his efforts to reform the Soviet Union; by 1989, historical forces proved too strong. The Berlin Wall tumbled, and Reagan's successor, George H. W. Bush, witnessed the disintegration of the Soviet Union. In a startling, surprising, and unexpected turn of events, the Cold War had ended.

After the Cold War, support for SDI diminished. As early as 1988, the new defense secretary, Frank Carlucci, ordered a steep reduction in SDIO expenditures. A year later the Bush administration officially declared a fully functional, leakproof missile defense impossible. Bush's defense secretary, John Tower, stated, "I don't believe that we can devise an umbrella that can protect the entire American population from nuclear incineration." Instead, the administration pursued Edward Teller's program of Brilliant Pebbles, which proposed sending thousands of missile interceptors with artificial intelligence into space.[9] Teller's dream remains unrealized, although the Bush administration tested ground-to-air missile defense in the first Iraq War, when Patriot interceptors destroyed Iraqi Scud missiles above Baghdad. Although not perfect, these successes in Iraq—made iconic with CNN news coverage—led Bush to proclaim in 1991 that SDI's mission would be refocused toward the "Global Protection Against Limited Strikes" (GPALS). It was a clear shift in priorities for a world with little threat of global thermonuclear war.

Despite Bush's appraisal of Star Wars, Reagan's most vociferous supporters, sometimes called the "Reagan Victory School," maintain their belief that

SDI was a form of economic warfare that drove the Soviets into economic submission—a view that remains highly contested. Whatever its role during the Cold War, as the national security scholar Rebecca Slayton has shown, SDI research remains important for its role in developing regional missile defense systems. By 2001, emboldened by the tragedy of September 11, the George W. Bush administration withdrew from the ABM Treaty, and in 2002 launched the Missile Defense Agency (MDA), a new version of the SDIO. Its focus would be defense against missile launch by rogue nuclear nations, such as North Korea. Bush's brazen promotion of these defenses, and his embrace of renewing nuclear "bunker-buster" bombs for tactical use, hearkened back to the tough talk of the hardliners of the first Reagan administration. As evidenced by Bush's cabinet, the Neocons were back.[10]

Just as SDI's legacy continued to be felt into the 2000s, Sagan's nuclear winter theory also remains relevant. In the 1980s, the public battle between Sagan and the defense establishment marked a trial run for future debates over climate change. Armed with scientific consensus, Sagan tried to convince the American people, and Congress, that the threat of nuclear winter proved the futility of the arms race. Repeatedly, Congress and administration officials acknowledged his warnings but ignored his policy suggestions. Some of Sagan's former associates see similar dynamics today. Brian Toon believes that in the 1980s "there were a whole bunch of people commenting on [nuclear winter, and] their knowledge of it was minimal. And you see the same thing going on now with global warming." Ann Druyan believes that Sagan's attempt to make "the consequences [of nuclear winter] real" was a strategy that since "has been duplicated many times by An Inconvenient Truth and others." So many years later, Sagan's former critics have also shifted focus; S. Fred Singer continues to criticize global warming science.[11] Seen in this context, the nuclear winter campaign hinted at environmental climate debates to come.

With his nuclear winter campaign of the 1980s, Sagan pleaded for disarmament; scientists today continue to push for arms reductions in a nuclear world. Richard Turco, Brian Toon, and Toon's collaborator Alan Robock continue to research and publish work on nuclear winter. Since 2007 they have contributed their findings to academic journals including Science, Atmospheric Chemistry and Physics, The National Academy of Sciences USA, and Physics Today. In a 2009 Scientific American article, "Local Nuclear War, Global Suffering," Toon and Robock warned that regional nuclear hotspots, including North Korea and the India-Pakistan border, run the risk of localized nuclear exchanges that, because of nuclear winter, would threaten world health and safety. These warnings are not falling on deaf ears. On February 9, 2009, President Barack Obama stressed, "It is important for the United States, in concert with Russia . . . to restart the conversations about how we can start reducing our nuclear arsenals in an effective way so that we then have standing to go to other countries and start stitching back together the nonproliferation treaties." Since that pronouncement, Obama has continued to crusade for an end to nuclear proliferation, attempting to work with Russia to rehash a new Strategic Arms Reduction Treaty that would reduce nuclear arsenals to their lowest levels since the 1950s. Recent saber-rattling between the two former superpowers, however, impinged that progress.[12]

With the breakup of the Soviet Union, the world let out a collective sigh of relief; after decades of living with "the bomb," we badly wanted to believe the nuclear threat was over. For generations born after 1991, the omnipresent threat of nuclear annihilation has been relegated to a bygone era, a fear as foreign and distant as polio. However much we want to ignore nuclear weapons, sadly, their threat is still real. As Richard Rhodes concludes in *The Twilight of the Bombs,* the potential of global thermonuclear war may have diminished after the Cold War, but the chance of isolated terrorist attacks with stolen warheads or "dirty bombs" remains.[13] Scientists continue to warn that a nuclear winter scenario is plausible, that any isolated or limited exchange might still doom citizens across the globe. That's a frightening prospect, especially considering the current pockets of tension and geopolitical hotspots that might trigger a nuclear exchange. Recent incidents on the India-Pakistan border as well as escalation of tensions between North Korea and its neighbors are but two examples of where limited nuclear war might lead to global devastation.

Since the 1990s, the global nuclear arsenal may have declined, but current levels are not insignificant. According to the nuclear watchdog *Bulletin of the Atomic Scientists,* as of 2016 the United States maintains a nuclear force of some 4,670 nuclear warheads, with close to 2,000 of those warheads currently deployed. Russia ranks second, with an estimated 4,500 warheads available for theater use and Vladimir Putin overseeing "a broad modernization of its strategic and nonstrategic nuclear forces." France, India, Israel, Pakistan, China, North Korea, and the United Kingdom all have "the bomb," with little checks on their use.[14] As former defense secretary Robert S. McNamara warned in the 2003 documentary *The Fog of War,* the use of these weapons is at the discretion not of any Congressional, Parliamentary, or international body, but by individual human beings—meaning that the arrival of an unhinged, reactionary leader in the United States would threaten to put the world at risk.

If there is a lesson to be learned by the efforts of antinuclear cultural activists, it is that in confronting nuclear weapons, popular culture matters. In the 1980s, writers, publishers, artists, directors, and scientists used their talents to turn political apathy into activism. Even if their efforts to support the freeze were manipulated by an administration committed to continuing the arms race, in time these efforts convinced leaders that their nuclear buildup was unpopular and allowed the administration to publicize a new commitment to preventing nuclear war. Today, activists do not need privileged access to television networks or printing houses; the age of social media has turned all of us into potential activists—as the Arab Spring, Occupy Wall St., and Black Lives Matter protests illustrate. Hopefully, before it is too late, similar efforts can be refocused towards confronting the ongoing, global, and deadly serious threat of nuclear weapons.

Notes

Introduction

1. James Kelly, "Thinking about the Unthinkable," *Time,* March 29, 1982, 12.
2. Allan Winkler, *Life Under a Cloud: American Anxiety about the Atom* (Oxford: Oxford University Press, 1993), 158; Tony Shaw, "Exposing America's Media–Energy Industry Complex during the Late Cold War: Hollywood's *The China Syndrome,*" and Natasha Zaretsky, "Atomic Nightmares and Biological Citizens at Three Mile Island," both papers presented at "Accidental Armageddons: The Nuclear Crisis and the Culture of the Second Cold War, 1975–1980" conference, German Historical Institute, Washington, DC, November 5, 2010.
3. Robert Collins, *Transforming America: Politics and Culture during the Reagan Years* (New York: Columbia University Press, 2007), 197–99; James Patterson, *Restless Giant: The United States from Watergate to Bush v. Gore* (Oxford: Oxford University Press, 2005), 123.
4. Frances FitzGerald, *Way Out There in the Blue: Reagan, Star Wars, and the End of the Cold War* (New York: Simon & Schuster, 2000), 74, 148.
5. Chester J. Pach, "Sticking to His Guns: Reagan and National Security," in *The Reagan Presidency: Pragmatic Conservatism and Its Legacies,* ed. W. Elliot Brownlee and Hugh Davis Graham (Lawrence: University Press of Kansas, 2003), 89–90.
6. Beth Fischer, *The Reagan Reversal: Foreign Policy and the End of the Cold War* (Columbia: University of Missouri Press, 2000), 4; John Lewis Gaddis, *Strategies of Containment: A Critical Appraisal of American National Security Policy during the Cold War,* rev. ed. (Oxford: Oxford University Press, 2005), 355–56; on Reagan's rhetoric and comparisons to earlier administrations, see Chester Pach, "The Reagan Doctrine: Principle, Pragmatism, and Policy" in *Presidential Studies Quarterly* 36.1 (March 2006): 77–79.
7. Robert Scheer, *With Enough Shovels: Reagan, Bush, and Nuclear War* (New York: Random House, 1982), 3–6, 18–19, 29; Colin S. Gray and Keith Paine, "Victory Is Possible," *Foreign Policy,* no. 39 (Summer 1980): 14–27.
8. Wilbur M. Smith, *This Atomic Age and the Word of God* (Boston: W. A. Wilde, 1948); on apocalyptic literature, see Paul Boyer, *Fallout: A Historian Reflects on America's Half-Century Encounter with Nuclear Weapons* (Columbus: Ohio State University Press, 1998), 130–38.
9. Ibid., 138–44.

10. Jerry Falwell, *Nuclear War and the Second Coming of Jesus Christ* (Lynchburg, VA: Old Time Gospel Hour, 1983), audiocassette; F. H. Knelman, *Reagan, God, and the Bomb: From Myth to Policy in the Nuclear Arms Race* (Buffalo, NY: Prometheus Books, 1985), 179–82.

11. Wade Green, "Rethinking the Unthinkable," *New York Times*, March 15, 1981; Gaddis Smith, "Reviews: *Life after Doomsday: A Survival Guide to Nuclear War and Other Major Disasters / Survive the Coming Nuclear War: How to Do It / Nuclear War Survival Skills / The Nuclear Survival Handbook*," *Bulletin of the Atomic Scientists* 39, no. 6 (June/ July 1983): 29–30.

12. Richard Rhodes, *Arsenals of Folly: The Making of the Nuclear Arms Race* (New York: Random House, 2007), 112; for a brief overview of the Neocons' rise, see George Packer, *The Assassins' Gate: America in Iraq* (New York: Farrar, Straus and Giroux, 2005), 15–24.

13. Rhodes, *Arsenals of Folly*, 118–21; Richard Pipes, *Vixi: Memoirs of a Non-Belonger* (New Haven, CT: Yale University Press, 2003), 136–44; Rhodes, *Arsenals of Folly*, 118–31; Daniel Wirls, *Buildup: The Politics of Defense in the Reagan Era* (Ithaca, NY: Cornell University Press, 1992), 22–23.

14. Pipes, *Vixi*, 141–43; Jeremi Suri, "Nuclear Weapons and the Escalation of Global Conflict since 1945," *International Journal* 63 (Autumn 2008): 1022; Richard Pipes, "Why the Soviet Union Thinks It Could Fight and Win a Nuclear War," *Commentary* 64.1 (July 1977): 21–35.

15. Rhodes, *Arsenals of Folly*, 144; Pipes's remarks taken from "Peace with Freedom: A Discussion by the Committee on the Present Danger before the Foreign Policy Association, 14 March 1978," quoted in *Alerting America: The Papers of the Committee on the Present Danger*, ed. Charles Tyroler II (Washington, DC: Pergamon-Brassey's, 1984), 25, 170–71; Patterson, *Restless Giant*, 123.

16. Reagan quote and budget totals found in Pach, "Sticking to His Guns," 90–95; see also Patterson, *Restless Giant*, 200; on defense budget, see Collins, *Transforming America*, 197; on MX and total defense expenditures, see Stephen I. Schwartz, ed., *Atomic Audit: The Costs and Consequences of U.S. Nuclear Weapons since 1940* (Washington, DC: Brookings Institution Press, 1998), 493–94.

17. George Herring, *From Colony to Superpower: US Foreign Relations since 1776* (New York: Oxford University Press, 2011), 863–66.

18. Lou Cannon, *President Reagan: The Role of a Lifetime* (New York: Public Affairs, 2000), 274–75; 1981 polling data found in Lawrence S. Wittner, *Toward Nuclear Abolition: A History of the World Nuclear Disarmament Movement, 1971–Present*, vol. 3 of *The Struggle against the Bomb*, (Stanford, CA: Stanford University Press, 2003), 170; 1983 polling data from Louis Harris, "Public Opinion and the Freeze Movement," *The Nuclear Weapons Freeze and Arms Control* (Cambridge, MA: Center for Science & International Affairs, 1983), 39; Harris poll cited in Rebecca S. Bjork, *The Strategic Defense Initiative: Symbolic Containment of the Nuclear Threat* (Albany: SUNY Press, 1992), 47–48.

19. "Who's Who in the Movement," *Newsweek*, April 26, 1982, 22; Robin Herman, "Anti-Nuclear Groups Are Using Professions as Rallying Points," *New York Times*, June 5, 1982.

20. Kyle Harvey, *American Anti-Nuclear Activism, 1975–1990: The Challenge of Peace* (New York: Palgrave Macmillan, 2014), 45–46.

21. Cortright quote from "A New Image for Antinuclear Lobby," *New York Times*, April 17,

1984; Helen Caldicott, *A Desperate Passion* (New York: W. W. Norton, 1997), 309; both quotes referenced in Harvey, *American Anti-Nuclear Activism,* 45–46, 54.

22. Wittner, *Toward Nuclear Abolition,* 173; Hedrick Smith, "The Nuclear Freeze," *New York Times,* April 1, 1982.

23. Wittner, *Toward Nuclear Abolition,* 175–77; David Cortright, *Peace Works* (Boulder, CO: Westview Press, 1993), 9–11; J. Michael Hogan, *The Nuclear Freeze Campaign: Rhetoric and Foreign Policy in the Telepolitical Age* (East Lansing: Michigan State University, 1994), 4.

24. Wittner, *Toward Nuclear Abolition,* 175–76.

25. Paul Boyer, *By the Bomb's Early Light: American Thought and Culture at the Dawn of the Atomic Age* (New York: Pantheon Books, 1985), xv.

26. Ibid., 360.

27. Boyer, *Fallout,* 167.

Chapter 1. Fear Books

1. Joann Davis and Wendy Smith, "A Checklist of Nuclear Books," *Publishers Weekly,* March 26, 1982, 45–51.

2. "Rethinking the Unthinkable," *New York Times,* March 15, 1981.

3. Robert Scheer, *With Enough Shovels: Reagan, Bush, and Nuclear War* (New York: Random House, 1982), 6–7.

4. Davis and Smith, "A Checklist of Nuclear Books," 45.

5. Ray Walters, "Paperback Talk," *New York Times,* April 25, 1982.

6. Lawrence S. Wittner, *Toward Nuclear Abolition: A History of the World Nuclear Disarmament Movement, 1971–Present,* vol. 3 of *The Struggle against the Bomb* (Stanford, CA: Stanford University Press, 2003), 1; Paul Boyer, *Fallout: A Historian Reflects on America's Half-Century Encounter with Nuclear Weapons* (Columbus: Ohio State University Press, 1998), 129.

7. Allan Winkler, *Life Under a Cloud: American Anxiety about the Atom* (New York: Oxford University Press, 1999), 158; Tony Shaw, "Exposing America's Media-Energy Industry Complex during the Late Cold War: Hollywood's *The China Syndrome,*" and Natasha Zaretsky, "Atomic Nightmares and Biological Citizens at Three Mile Island," both papers presented at "Accidental Armageddons: The Nuclear Crisis and the Culture of the Second Cold War, 1975–1980" conference, German Historical Institute, Washington, DC, November 5, 2010.

8. Tom Engelhardt, Skype interview by the author, January 21, 2011.

9. Ibid.

10. Specifically, the call for drawings translates as "Let Us Leave for Posterity Pictures of the Atomic Bomb Drawn by Citizens." Japan Broadcasting Corporation, ed., *The Unforgettable Fire: Pictures Drawn by Atomic Bomb Survivors* (New York: Pantheon, 1981), 5, 105–9.

11. Engelhardt interview; John Hersey quoted on cover of *The Unforgettable Fire;* Herbert Mitgang, "Bomb Watchers," *New York Times,* August 21, 1981.

12. Engelhardt interview.

13. Matthew L. Wald, "Memories from 1945 Live as Art," *New York Times,* August 11, 1985.

14. Nathaniel Sheppard Jr., "Museum in Chicago Focuses on Peace," *New York Times,* August 8, 1982; Eamon Dunphy, *The Unforgettable Fire: The Story of U2* (New York:

Penguin Books, 1987), 295; Hank Bordowitz, ed., *The U2 Reader: A Quarter Century of Commentary, Criticism, and Reviews* (Milwaukee, WI: Hal Leonard, 2003), 47.

15. James Reston, "Washington: Reagan's Forgotten Issue: The Growing Outcry Over Nuclear Arms Race," *Lawrence (KS) Journal-World,* March 26, 1982.

16. Wittner, *Toward Nuclear Abolition,* 172–75; Mary McGrory, "If the Bomb Dropped at 3 p.m. Monday . . . Think About It," *Washington Post,* February 18, 1982.

17. Fred Kaplan, *The Wizards of Armageddon* (Stanford: Stanford University Press, 1983).

18. "Books of the Times," *New York Times,* April 8, 1982.

19. Jonathan Schell, *The Fate of the Earth and The Abolition* (Stanford: Stanford University Press, 2000), 43–44.

20. Ibid., 39, 60.

21. Peter McGrath, "The Nuclear Book Boom," *Newsweek,* April 12, 1982, 21.

22. The cost price in 1982 was about $2.25. Davis and Smith, "A Checklist of Nuclear Books," 45–51.

23. Lardner, "The Bomb Schell."

24. Ibid.; Michele Slung, "Nuclear Fears," *Washington Post,* February 28, 1982; "Best Sellers: Nonfiction," *New York Times,* May 9, 1982.

25. Moyers quoted in Philip M. Boffey, "Contemplating the Heart of the Nuclear Darkness," *New York Times,* March 28, 1982; Caldicott quoted in James Lardner, "The Bomb Schell: The Media Fallout after *The Fate of the Earth,*" *Washington Post,* April 22, 1982.

26. Mondale quote found in Lardner, "The Bomb Schell."

27. *WSJ,* Guthe, and Payne quotes found in Boffey, "Contemplating the Heart of the Nuclear Darkness."

28. Quotes from the "Editorial Desk" in "How Much Is Enough?," *New York Times,* April 11, 1982.

29. Ibid.

30. Maud Marshall, "Nuclear Weapons Are the Enemy," letter to the editor, *New York Times,* April 22, 1982.

31. Reston, "Reagan's Forgotten Issue"; Melvin Maddocks, "Marching against Calamity," *Christian Science Monitor,* April 26, 1982; Boyer, *By the Bomb's Early Light,* 364.

32. Douglas Martin, "Roger C. Molander, Nuclear Protest Leader, Dies at 71," *New York Times,* March 31, 2012.

33. Molander quote from "Briefing," *New York Times,* October 20, 1981.

34. Rushworth M. Kidder, "Growing Numbers Support US Nuclear Disarmament," *Christian Science Monitor,* November 3, 1981; Spencer Weart, *Nuclear Fear: A History of Images* (Cambridge, MA: Harvard University Press, 1988), 386–88; Gallup Poll data from "Disarmament Movement Could Become Top Popular Cause," *Santa Cruz Sentinel,* November 15, 1981.

35. "Briefing," *New York Times,* October 20, 1981.

36. Ground Zero, *Nuclear War,* 13–14.

37. Molander's "Dr. Strangelove" quote found in "Disarmament Movement Could Become Top Popular Cause," *Santa Cruz Sentinel,* November 15, 1981; also reprinted in Kidder, "Growing Numbers Support US Nuclear Disarmament."

38. Martin Asher quoted in Walters, "Paperback Talk."

39. Ibid.

40. David S. Broder, "Cheapening the Nuclear Debate," *Washington Post,* May 2, 1982.

41. Sandra Martin, "Paperbacks: The Problems Inherent in the Deluge of Rhetoric in the Nuclear Age: Perspective Is Everything," *Globe and Mail* (Toronto, ON), May 15, 1982.

42. "Ground Zero Week," *Christian Science Monitor,* editorial, April 20, 1982; Melvin Maddocks, "Marching Against Calamity," *Christian Science Monitor,* April 26, 1982.

43. "Experts to Field Questions on TV for 'Ground Zero,'" *Christian Science Monitor,* April 22, 1982.

44. "Ground Zero Week" pamphlet and materials archived in file "Nuclear Freeze," folder 3 of 8, box OA 10529, David Gergen Files, Ronald Reagan Library.

45. "Congress's Moratorium Proposal and the Administration's Reply," *New York Times,* March 21, 1982.

46. Walters, "Paperback Talk"; Peter deLeon, "Freeze: The Literature of the Nuclear Weapons Debate," *Journal of Conflict Resolution* 27.1 (March 1983): 182–83.

47. Edward M. Kennedy and Mark O. Hatfield, *Freeze! How You Can Help Prevent Nuclear War* (London: Bantam, 1982).

48. Broder, "Cheapening the Nuclear Debate."

49. "WNYC Covers the Great Anti-Nuclear March and Rally at Central Park, June 12, 1982," audio archived online at www.wnyc.org/story/wnyc-covers-great-anti-nuclear-march-and-rally-central-park-june-12-1982/.

50. Douglas C. Waller, *Congress and the Nuclear Freeze: An Inside Look at the Politics of a Mass Movement* (Amherst: University of Massachusetts Press, 1987), 162–63.

51. Scheer, *With Enough Shovels,* 7.

52. Waller, *Congress and the Nuclear Freeze,* 162–63.

53. "Congress's Moratorium Proposal and the Administration's Reply," *New York Times* March 21, 1982.

54. Memo, Jim Cicconi to James Baker, "A Couple Thoughts on the Nuclear Freeze / Arms Reduction Statement We Are Now Considering," March 30, 1982, file "Nuclear Freeze," folder 3 of 8, box OA 10529, David Gergen Files, Ronald Reagan Library.

55. Collins, *Transforming America,* 197–99; on the Euromissiles, see Samuel F. Wells Jr., "Reagan, Euromissiles, and Europe," in *The Reagan Presidency: Pragmatic Conservatism and Its Legacies,* ed. W. Elliot Brownlee and Hugh David Graham (Lawrence: University Press of Kansas, 2003), 133–54.

56. Flora Lewis, "Brezhnev's Missile Freeze Is Still Far from a Thaw," *New York Times,* March 21, 1982.

57. Cicconi, "A Couple Thoughts."

58. Memo, Red Cavaney to Michael Deaver,, "Nuclear Freeze (January–June 1982 [2 of 3])," memo Subject Files 1981–1983, box 26, OA 6390, Elizabeth H. Dole Files, Ronald Reagan Library.

59. Memo, William Clark to Edwin Meese, James Baker, and Michael Deaver, "Policy Offensive on Arms Control and the Anti-Nuclear Movement," April 22, 1982, folder "Nuclear Freeze," 1 of 8, box OA 10529, WHORM: Subject File, David Gergen Files, Ronald Reagan Library.

60. Ibid.

61. Ibid.

62. Ibid.

63. Ibid.

64. Ibid.

65. William Clark to Secretaries of State and Defense and Directors of Arms Control and Disarmament Agency / International Communication Agency, April 26, 1982, "Nuclear Freeze," folder1 of 8, box OA 10529, WHORM: Subject File, David Gergen Files, Ronald Reagan Library.

66. Ibid.
67. William Hubert Lewis et al., *In Search of Peace: American Initiatives, 1946–1982* (United States International Communication Agency, 1982); Reagan's proposed response found in Robert "Bud" McFarlane memo to David R. Gergen, "Position on Freeze," March 24, 1982, "Nuclear Freeze," folder 3 of 8, box OA 10529, WHORM: Subject File, David Gergen Files, Ronald Reagan Library.
68. Memo, Dave Gergen to Jim Baker, "Public Affairs Group on Nuclear Issues," May 28, 1982, "Nuclear Freeze," folder 4 of 8, box OA 10529, WHORM: Subject File, David Gergen Files, Ronald Reagan Library.
69. Ibid.
70. US Department of State, "Proposed National Media Strategy for Arms Control Policy," folder "Nuclear Freeze" (6 of 8), box OA 10529, WHORM: Subject File, David Gergen Files, Ronald Reagan Library.
71. Edwin McDowell, "Nuclear Books Proliferating, but Few Sell Well," *New York Times*, November 4, 1982.
72. J. Michael Hogan, *The Nuclear Freeze Campaign: Rhetoric and Foreign Policy in the Telepolitical Age* (East Lansing: Michigan State University, 1994), 4.

Chapter 2. The Nuclear Winter

1. The nuclear winter hypothesis is summarized nicely in Paul Ehrlich et al., *The Cold and the Dark: The World after Nuclear War* (New York: W. W. Norton, 1984), 3–4; Carl Sagan and Richard Turco, *A Path Where No Man Thought: Nuclear Winter and the End of the Arms Race* (New York: Random House, 1990), 39, 95–101.
2. Keay Davidson, *Carl Sagan: A Life* (New York: John Wiley & Sons, 1999), 354–380; William Poundstone, *Carl Sagan: A Life in the Cosmos* (New York: Henry Holt, 1999), 292–323.
3. Paul Rubinson, "The Global Effects of Nuclear Winter: Science and Antinuclear Protest in the United States and the Soviet Union during the 1980s," *Cold War History* 14.1 (February 2014): 47–69.
4. Lawrence Badash, *A Nuclear Winter's Tale: Science and Politics in the 1980s* (Cambridge, MA: MIT Press, 2009), xi–xii.
5. Allan D. Brandt, *The Cigarette Century: The Rise, Fall, and Deadly Persistence of the Product That Defined America* (New York: Basic Books, 2009), 204.
6. Matthias Dörries, "The Politics of Atmospheric Sciences: 'Nuclear Winter' and Global Climate Change," *Osiris* 26.1 (2011): 198–223; Naomi Oreskes and Erik M. Conway, *Merchants of Doubt: How a Handful of Scientists Obscured the Truth on Issues from Tobacco Smoke to Global Warming* (New York: Bloomsbury Press, 2011), 36–65; Wilfried Mausbach, "Nuclear Winter: Prophecies of Doom and Images of Desolation during the Second Cold War," in *Nuclear Threats, Nuclear Fear, and the Cold War of the 1980s*, ed. Eckart Conze, Martin Klimke, and Jeremy Varon (New York: Cambridge University Press, 2016).
7. For an example of nuclear winter scientific debates, see Starley L. Thompson and Stephen H. Schneider, "Nuclear Winter Reappraised," *Foreign Affairs* 64 (1986): 981–1005; note that two historians of the subject, Badash and Rubinson, both consider nuclear winter a legitimate scientific theory.
8. Sagan's early life is covered succinctly in Dörries, "The Politics of Atmospheric

Sciences," 209; for quotes regarding Sagan and science fiction, see Davidson, *Carl Sagan*, 218, and Poundstone, *Carl Sagan*, 12.

9. "Enormous interest" quote attributed to Sagan's friend Peter Pesch, quoted in Davidson, *Carl Sagan*, 37.

10. Paul Boyer, *By the Bomb's Early Light: American Thought and Culture at the Dawn of the Atomic Age* (New York: Pantheon Books, 1985), 115, 257.

11. On bomb shelters in American culture, see Elaine Tyler May, *Homeward Bound: American Families in the Cold War Era* (New York: Basic Books, 1999) 3–5, 92–113; see also Laura McEnaney, *Civil Defense Begins at Home: Militarization Meets Everyday Life in the Fifties* (Princeton, NJ: Princeton University Press, 2000).

12. Christopher Anvil, "Torch," *Astounding Science Fiction*, April 1957, 41–50; "Feedback," *New Scientist*, March 5, 1987, 55; "Christopher Anvil" was the pen name of Harry C. Crosby, who began writing short stories in the early 1950s. By 1956, Anvil's stories appeared alongside the work of other popular sci-fi writers including Arthur C. Clarke and Raymond F. Jones; see Eric Flint, ed., *Christopher Anvil: War Games* (Riverdale, NY: Baen Publishers, 2010).

13. Ron Miller and Frederick C. Durant III, eds., *The Art of Chesley Bonestell* (London: Paper Tiger, 2001), 9. Sagan's widow Ann Druyan confirmed his Bonestell collection. Druyan, Skype interview by the author, February 8, 2011.

14. Robert M. Richardson, "Rocket Blitz from the Moon," *Collier's*, October 23, 1948, 23–25, 44–46. Few noticed the connections between sci-fi and Sagan's theory; see Thompson and Schneider, "Nuclear Winter Reappraised," 984, including footnote.

15. Dörries, "The Politics of Atmospheric Sciences," 209–10.

16. On the 1960s divide between science and society, see Matt Tribbe, *No Requiem for the Space Age* (New York: Oxford University Press, 2014); Rubinson, "Containing Science," 66–109; on Sagan and Pauling, see Davidson, *Carl Sagan*, 64–65.

17. Carl Sagan, *Pale Blue Dot: A Vision of Human Future in Space* (New York: Ballantine Books, 1994), 174; President Richard Nixon, "Special Message to the Congress Outlining the 1972 Environmental Program," February 8, 1972, available at *The American Presidency Project*, Public Papers of the Presidents, ed. John T. Woolley and Gerhard Peters, UC Santa Barbara, www.presidency.ucsb.edu/ws/?pid=3731.

18. On Sagan's rising popularity, see Davidson, *Carl Sagan: A Life*, 260–65; Carter quote from Douglas Brinkley, *The Unfinished Presidency: Jimmy Carter's Journey beyond the White House* (New York: Viking, 1998), 32.

19. Poundstone, *Carl Sagan*, 155–56.

20. Sagan and Turco, *A Path Where No Man Thought*, 455–56.

21. On Tambora, see ibid., 456–60.

22. Luis W. Alvarez et al., "Extraterrestrial Cause for the Cretaceous-Tertiary Extinction," *Science*, June 6, 1980, 1095–108; Badash, *A Nuclear Winter's Tale*, 42–43.

23. Badash, *A Nuclear Winter's Tale*, 49–62; Sagan et al., *The Cold and the Dark*, xiii–xv.

24. The Ambio findings are summarized in *The Aftermath: The Human and Ecological Consequences of Nuclear War*, ed. Jeannie Peterson (New York: Pantheon Books, 1983), 4–78.

25. Hark A. Harwell, *Nuclear Winter: The Human and Environmental Consequences of Nuclear War* (New York: Springer-Verlag, 1984), viii; Poundstone, *Carl Sagan*, 293–99.

26. On Sagan's rising popularity, see Davidson, *Carl Sagan*, 107, 114–17; on Sagan's publishing in *Parade*, see Badash, *A Nuclear Winter's Tale*, 66; on Sagan's scholarly output, see Poundstone, *Carl Sagan*, 288–89.

27. Richard Turco, Skype interview by the author, February 2, 2011.

28. On atomic culture, see Spencer Weart, *The Rise of Nuclear Fear* (Cambridge, MA: Harvard University Press, 2012), 123–37.

29. William A. Ausmus, "Pragmatic Uses of Metaphor: Models and Metaphor in the Nuclear Winter Scenario," *Communication Monographs* 65 (March 1998): 69–71.

30. Poundstone, *Carl Sagan*, 305.

31. Harwell, *Nuclear Winter*, viii–ix; Sagan and Turco, *A Place Where No Man Thought*, 20–21.

32. Paul Ehrlich, *The Population Bomb* (New York: Ballantine Books, 1968). Ehrlich's population control thesis remains controversial: see Matthew Connelly, *Fatal Misconceptions: The Struggle to Control World Population* (New York: Belknap Press, 2008); Paul R. Ehrlich and Anne H. Ehrlich, "The Population Bomb Revisited," *Electronic Journal of Sustainable Development* 1.3 (2009): 63–71.

33. Paul R. Ehrlich, "Disarmament: The Lesser Risk," *Bulletin of the Atomic Scientists* 38.7 (August/September 1982): 7–8.

34. H. Lewis, "How 'Nuclear Winter' Got on Page One," *Newsletter of the National Association of Science Writers* 32.2 (April 1984): 7–8 (hereafter *NNASW*).

35. Badash, *A Nuclear Winter's Tale*, 65–66.

36. Ibid., 49–76, Rathjen quote on 83; Rubinson, "Containing Science," 293–95.

37. *NNASW.*

38. Ibid.

39. On NASA funding, see Jeffrey Zaslow, "Report on Business," *Wall Street Journal*, September 14, 2001.

40. Dorothy Nelkin, *Selling Science: How the Press Covers Science and Technology* (New York: W. H. Freeman, 1995), 159–71.

41. Rob Wood and Pamela Ronsaville, Skype interview by the author, January 21, 2011.

42. Ibid.; Ehrlich et al., *The Cold and the Dark*, 60–61.

43. Jon Lomberg, interview by the author, January 18, 2011; Davidson, *Carl Sagan*, 303; Walter Anderson, "Science and the Press," in *Carl Sagan's Universe*, ed. Tervant Terzian and Elizabeth Bilson (New York: Cambridge University Press, 1997), 207–9; *Parade Magazine*, October 30, 1983; Paul Ehrlich, "Nuclear Winter: The Inside Story," *CoEvolution Quarterly*, no. 42 (Summer 1984): 88–94.

44. *The Global Environmental Consequences of Nuclear War*, 1983, DVD copy, provided to the author by Bob Derkash.

45. Druyan, Skype interview.

46. Carl Sagan et al., "Nuclear Winter: Global Consequences of Multiple Nuclear Explosions," *Science*, December 23, 1983, 1283–292; Carl Sagan, "Nuclear War and Climatic Catastrophe: Some Policy Implications," *Foreign Affairs* 62.2 (Winter 1983/1984): 257–92; *NNASW.*

47. On publicity from *Parade*, see Anderson, "Science and the Press," 208.

48. George C. Herring, *From Colony to Superpower: U.S. Foreign Relations since 1776* (Oxford: Oxford University Press, 2008), 888–89.

49. *NNASW.*

50. *NNASW.*

51. Druyan, Skype interview; *Time* cover archived online at http://content.time.com/time/covers/0,16641,19840102,00.html.

52. Badash, *A Nuclear Winter's Tale*, 101–2; portions of the *Nightline* transcript found in Bob Sims to Dave Gergen, "Material for Today's 4:00 PM Meeting on 'The Day After,'"

November 3, 1983, folder "Nuclear Weapons Effects," box 90427, Ronald Lehman Files, Ronald Reagan Library.

53. In an overall magisterial work, Herring makes one minor error, stating that ABC aired *The Day After* on November 11 (*From Colony to Superpower*, 861); on Sagan's friendship with Koppel: Druyan, Skype interview..

54. ABC News, *Viewpoint*, November 20, 1983, accessed at Vanderbilt Television News Archive, transcribed by the author; portions of the program are now available on YouTube.

55. Ibid.; Druyan, Skype interview.

56. Jon Lomberg, e-mail to the author, December 28, 2010.

57. CBS, *Face the Nation*, December 14, 1984, transcript found in Ronald Lehman Papers, "Nuclear Winter," File: 905–40, WHORM: Subject File, Ronald Reagan Library.

58. Druyan, Skype interview; Jon Lomberg, Skype interview with the author, February 2, 2011; Lomberg made similar claims about the impact of nuclear winter in "The Visual Presentation of Science," in Terzian and Bilson, *Carl Sagan's Universe*, 202–3.

59. "Statement by the Honourable David Lange, Prime Minster of New Zealand," September 25, 1984, White House Office File, European and Soviet Affairs Directorate, National Security Council, box 910337, folder "Nuclear Winter," Ronald Reagan Library.

60. "Memorandum for Mr. John M. Fisher, Page 3," a single-page document (that was perhaps misfiled) and part of a longer memo, with handwritten note reading "New File JL Nuclear Winter," found ibid.

61. *Congressional Record—Senate* 130 (22 May 1984), S13141–S13142, cited in Badash, *A Nuclear Winter's Tale*, 128.

62. Ibid., 131; *The Consequences of Nuclear War: Hearings before the Subcommittee on International Trade, Finance, and Security Economics of the Joint Economic Committee, Congress of the United States, Ninety-eighth Congress, Second Session, July 11 and 12, 1984* (Washington, DC: GPO, 1986).

63. Badash, *A Nuclear Winter's Tale*, 133; *The Climatic, Biological, and Strategic Effects of Nuclear War: Hearing before the Subcommittee on Natural Resources, Agriculture Research, and Environment of the Committee on Science and Technology, House of Representatives, Ninety-eighth Congress, Second Session, September 12, 1984* (Washington, DC: GPO, 1985).

64. Maddox quote from Richard P. Turco et al., " 'Nuclear Winter' to Be Taken seriously," *Nature*, September 27, 1984, 307; on nuclear winter debates in scientific journals, see Badash, *A Nuclear Winter's Tale*, chap. 14.

65. Carl Sagan, "Nuclear War and Climatic Catastrophe: Some Policy Implications," *Foreign Affairs* 62 (Winter 1983): 276, 292.

66. "Transcript of Interview with President on a Range of Issues," *New York Times*, February 12, 1985; quote appears in Badash, *A Nuclear Winter's Tale*, 163.

67. Caspar W. Weinberger, "The Potential Effects of Nuclear War on the Climate: A Report to the United States Congress," March 1985, in *Nuclear Winter and Its Implications*, Hearings of Senate Armed Services Committee, 99th Cong., 1st sess., October 2–3, 1985 (Washington, DC: GPO, 1985), 9–15.

68. Reported by Connie Chung, *NBC Nightly News*, March 2, 1985, accessed at Vanderbilt Television News Archive.

69. Timothy Wirth quoted in M. Weisskopf, "Pentagon Says Nuclear Winter Justifies Arms," *Washington Post*, March 3, 1985; Badash, *A Nuclear Winter's Tale*, 165.

70. Starley L. Thompson and Stephen H. Schneider, "Nuclear Winter Reappraised," *Foreign Affairs* 64.5 (Summer 1986): 981–1005; Carl Sagan, "Comment and Correspondence: The Nuclear Winter Debate," *Foreign Affairs* 65.1 (Fall 1986): 163–68; Badash, *A Nuclear Winter's Tale,* 118–24.

71. Carl Sagan, "Nuclear Winter: Changing Our Way of Thinking," speech at Harvard University, recorded by Eschaton Foundation, Educational Film & Video Project, Berkeley, CA, 1985, videocassette.

72. Russell Seitz, "Comment and Correspondence," *Foreign Affairs* 62.4 (Spring 1984): 995–1002; Oreskes and Conway, *Merchants of Doubt,* 25–27.

73. Despite published criticisms from Richard Turco, Seitz did have an affiliation with Harvard in the mid-1980s; credentials are examined in Brian Martin, "Nuclear Winter: Science and Politics" in *Science and Public Policy,* Vol. 15, No. 5 (October 1988): 321–34.

74. Brian Toon, Skype interview by the author, January 25, 2011; Patrick Clawson, Edward N. Luttwak, and Russell Seitz, "Comment and Correspondence: Nuclear Winter," *Foreign Affairs* 62.4 (Spring 1984): 997–99; Badash, *A Nuclear Winter's Tale,* 122–24.

75. On Seitz, see Oreskes and Conway, *Merchants of Doubt,* 25–27; Sagan's suspicions related by Toon, Skype interview.

76. Brad Sparks, "The Scandal of Nuclear Winter," *National Review,* November 15, 1985, 35–38.

77. Russell Seitz, "In from the Cold: 'Nuclear Winter' Melts Down," *National Interest,* no. 5 (Fall 1986): 3–17; Howard Maccabee, "Nuclear Winter: How Much Do We Really Know?," *Reason* 17.1 (May 1985): 28.

78. Russell Seitz, "Is the 'Nuclear Winter' Real?," *Nature,* August 23, 1984, 625; this and other articles critiquing nuclear winter found in S. Fred Singer note to George Keyworth, August 20, 1984, "Nuclear Winter Meeting—Erice, Italy," which included Singer's January 12, 1984, letter to the editor of *Science* as well as Singer's report "Nuclear Winter on the Day After," November 25, 1983; folder "Nuclear Winter," file 4 of 4, George Keyworth Files, Ronald Reagan Library.

79. Russell Seitz, "The Apocryphal Apocalypse: 'Nuclear Winter' Environmental Surrealism and Video Gamesmanship," p. 9, White House Office File, European and Soviet Affairs Directorate, National Security Council, box 91037, folder "Nuclear Winter," Ronald Reagan Library.

80. In interviews conducted by the author, these artists maintain that Seitz quoted them out of context. Wood and Ronsaville, Skype interview; Lomberg, Skype interview, February 2, 2011; Seitz, "The Apocryphal Apocalypse, p. 00."

81. Seitz, "The Apocryphal Apocalypse," p. 14.

82. Druyan, Skype interview; Seitz, "The Apocryphal Apocalypse," p. 15, but Seitz was incorrect about the funding amount, estimated by Jack Porter to be around $100,000; see *NNASW.*

83. Seitz's credentials are listed on the cover page of "The Apocryphal Apocalypse"; for other examples of attacking scientific findings at odds with the arms race, see Russell Seitz, "Direct Injection of Carbon: The Stratosphere, Fireballs, Fossil Fuel" and "The Book of the Apocalypse," White House Office File, European and Soviet Affairs Directorate, National Security Council, box 91037, folder "Nuclear Winter," Ronald Reagan Library.

84. S. Fred Singer, "Freedom of the Seas and Nuclear Winter," February 14, 1985, found ibid.

85. Reagan quoted in Robert C. Tucker, "Keeping Peace between the Superpowers: Toward a Cooperative Regime of War Prevention," *Princeton Alumni Weekly,* November 6, 1985, 23.

86. Russell Seitz, "An Incomplete Obituary," *Forbes,* February 10, 1997, 123.

87. Druyan, Skype interview.

88. Gorbachev quoted in Mark Hertsgaard, "Mikhail Gorbachev Explains What's Rotten in Russia," *Salon.com,* September 7, 2000, www.salon.com/2000/09/07/gorbachev; see Rubinson, "The Global Effects of Nuclear Winter: Science and Antinuclear Protest in the United States and the Soviet Union during the 1980s," *Cold War History* 14.1 (2014): 69.

89. Badash, *A Nuclear Winter's Tale,* 173.

Chapter 3. Containing *The Day After*

1. Reagan and Gromyko quoted in Dan Oberdorfer, *The Turn: From the Cold War to a New Era* (New York: Poseidon Press, 1991), 59–61; on state of global affairs, see Lou Cannon, *President Reagan: The Role of a Lifetime* (New York: Public Affairs, 2000), 274–75.

2. George C. Herring, *From Colony to Superpower: U.S. Foreign Relations since 1776* (New York: Oxford University Press, 2008), 872–73; Cannon, *President Reagan,* 385–89.

3. Samuel F. Wells Jr., "Reagan, Euromissiles, and Europe," in *The Reagan Presidency: Pragmatic Conservatism and Its Legacies,* ed. W. Elliot Brownlee and Hugh David Graham (Lawrence: University Press of Kansas, 2003); Richard Rhodes, *Arsenals of Folly: The Making of the Nuclear Arms Race* (New York: Random House, 2007), 154–55.

4. Robert Collins, *Transforming America: Politics and Culture in the Reagan Years* (New York: Columbia University Press, 2007), 197–99; for an overview on the Euromissiles, see Wells Jr., "Reagan, Euromissiles, and Europe," 133–54.

5. On 1980s antinuclear films, see William J. Palmer, *The Films of the Eighties: A Social History* (Carbondale: Southern Illinois University Press, 1995), 179–206; on *The Day After* as being the biggest media event of the year, see Toni A. Perrine, *Film and the Nuclear Age: Representing Cultural Anxiety* (New York: Garland, 1998), 153–54.

6. There were other depictions of nuclear war on television including CBS's five-part documentary *The Defense of the United States;* NBC had two nuclear-themed films in the early 1980s: *World War III* (1982) and the Emmy Award–winning *Special Bulletin* (1983). See Tom Shales, "*The Day After* Approaches," *Washington Post,* October 11, 1983.

7. John Corry, "'The Day After': TV as a Rallying Cry," *New York Times,* November 20, 1983; memo, Kevin R. Hopkins to Edwin Meese, November 3, 1983, ID#183992, PR016–01, WHORM: Subject File, Ronald Reagan Library.

8. Edward Hume quote from CBS, *60 Minutes,* November 13, 1983, transcript of program found in Jude Muskett memo to Dave Gergen, November 17, 1983, folder "The Day After," box OA 10522, David Gergen Files, Ronald Reagan Library.

9. Nicholas Meyer quotes from Stephen Farber, "How a Nuclear Holocaust Was Staged for TV," *New York Times,* November 13, 1983; Harry F. Waters et al., "TV's Nuclear Nightmare," *Newsweek,* November 21, 1983, 66–72.

10. Mick Broderick, *Nuclear Movies: A Critical Analysis and Filmography of International Feature Length Films Dealing with Experimentation, Aliens, Terrorism, Holocaust, and Other Disaster Scenarios, 1914–1989* (Jefferson, NC: McFarland, 1991), 41.

11. Nicholas Meyer, *The View from the Bridge: Memories of Star Trek and a Life in Hollywood* (New York: Viking, 2009), 139–44, 151.

12. Meyer quote from "America Is Hit: 'The Day After' Brings Nuclear War Horror . . . and Hot Controversy," *TV Guide,* November 19–25, 1983, 6.

13. Meyer quote from Susan Boyd-Bowman, "'The Day After': Representations of the Nuclear Holocaust," *Screen* 25.4–5 (July–October 1984): 74.

14. Ibid.; NPR, *All Things Considered*, October 13, 1983, transcript provided by "Radio TV Reports, Inc.," included in folder "The Day After," box OA 9118, Karna Small-Stringer Files, Ronald Reagan Library.

15. "Piece of cake": attributed to Richard Grenier, "The Brandon Stoddard Horror Show," *National Review*, December 9, 1983, 1553; *New York Post* op-ed quoted in Wittner, *Toward Nuclear Abolition*, 187.

16. Letter, Daniel O. Graham to Karna Small, November 4, 1983, with attachment "High Frontier: Two Day Media Blitz, November 20, 21, 1983—Response to *The Day After*," ID# 183666, PR016–01, WHORM: Subject File, Ronald Reagan Library.

17. Sally Bedell Smith, "ABC to Show Nuclear War Drama in November," *New York Times*, September 3, 1983.

18. Edward Gorman, "Day After Blitzed US Ratings," *Broadcast*, November 25, 1983, 6; "High Frontier: Two Day Media Blitz."

19. "ABC-TV Backs Deterrence," *National Review*, October 11, 1983, 1183; Reed Irving, "ABC's Nuclear Horror Movie," *Washington Times*, October 18, 1983; "High Frontier: Two Day Media Blitz."

20. Memo, Robert B. Sims to Robert C. McFarlane and David Gergen, November 9, 1983, folder "The Day After (3 of 5)," box 15, Karna Small-Stringer Files, Ronald Reagan Library; Everett H. Erlick to Charles Wick, October 7, 1983, ID# 16780655, PR016–01, WHORM: Subject File, Ronald Reagan Library.

21. John Corry, "'The Crisis Game' Simulates War Debate," *New York Times*, November 22, 1983.

22. Boyd-Bowman, "'The Day After,'" 81; Meyer, *The View from the Bridge*, 152; Wittner, *Toward Nuclear Abolition*, 266–67.

23. "Draft: Public Affairs Plan: '*The Day After*,'" folder "ABC's 'The Day After' 11/20/1983 (5 of 5)," box OA 9118, Karna Small-Stringer files, Ronald Reagan Library; this draft was also distributed in Confidential Memo, Robert Sims to David Gergen, Ron Lehman, Sven Kraemer, and Ray Pollock, November 3, 1983, folder "Nuclear Weapons Effects," box 90427, Ronald Lehman Files, Ronald Reagan Library.

24. Sims to McFarlane and Gergen memo.

25. "Excerpts from the President's Speech in Japan," *New York Times*, November 11, 1983; the White House strategy to use this language can be found on page 2, bullet point 3, of the finalized "Public Affairs Strategy for '*The Day After*,'" folder "ABC's 'The Day After' 11/20/1983 (5 of 5)."

26. "Draft: Public Affairs Plan"; there is no date given in the meeting notes, but notes for a meeting dated November 4, 1983, seem similar: "handwritten notes filed by Office of Policy Development concerning ABC-TV film *The Day After*," ID#183993, PR016–01, WHORM: Subject File, Ronald Reagan Library; the actual "Notes from Meeting on '*The Day After*'" are in folder "ABC's 'The Day After' 11/20/1983 (4 of 5)."

27. "Notes from Meeting on '*The Day After*'"; Sims to McFarlane and Gergen memo.

28. On staffing the phones, see "Draft: Public Affairs Plan," 14; on the tally of "twenty" additional operators, see memo, David R. Gergen to the President, November 21, 1983, folder "ABC's 'The Day After' 11/20/1983 (1 of 5)."

29. "Talking Points for Answering Calls After 'The Day After' Sunday Evening," folder "ABC's 'The Day After' 11/20/1983 (2 of 5)."

30. George H. W. Bush, "Preserving Peace through Deterrence," *New York Times,* November 21, 1983.

31. "Selected Activities Involving DOD Officials, November 17–25, 1983," folder "ABC's 'The Day After' 11/20/1983 (3 of 5)"; an edited version of Weinberger's op-ed piece is included in folder (2 of 5).

32. Dr. G. A. Keyworth, Science Advisor to the President, "Which Way to Prevent Nuclear War?," op-ed, folder "*The Day After,*" box OA 11691, Bruce Chapman Files, Ronald Reagan Library.

33. Gergen to the President memo.

34. Ibid.

35. Sue to Karna Small, "Talk Show Requests," November 17, 1983, folder "ABC's 'The Day After' 11/20/1983 (5 of 5)." The American Legion lawsuit was brought up by "DG," likely David Gergen, in a misplaced meeting minute note found immediately after the document. Gergen quote from "Notes from Meeting on 'The Day After,'" bullet point 12.

36. Memo, William I. Greener to David R. Gergen, November 17, 1983, box OA 10132, David Gergen Files, Ronald Reagan Library.

37. Founded in 1983, CFA later gained notoriety for aiding Col. Oliver North in the Iran-Contra scandal. Lew Lehrman to Chairman, and "Citizens for America: Call for Action" packet, both dated November 15, 1983, folder "ABC's 'The Day After' 11/20/1983 (4 of 5)"; "Draft: Public Affairs Plan."

38. Ibid.

39. "High Frontier: Two Day Media Blitz," not to be confused with the "Draft: Public Affairs Plan," which was the official draft of White House plans to contain *The Day After;* Graham's plan is also included in Daniel O. Graham to Karna Small, November 4, 1983, folder "ABC's 'The Day After' 11/20/1983 (4 of 5)."

40. Ibid. No ads by any organization or sponsor ran during *The Day After.*

41. Ibid.

42. Memo, David B. Waller to Fred F. Fielding, November 14, 1983, and letter, Edwin Meese III to Daniel O. Graham, December 9, 1983, both in ID#183666, PR016–01, WHORM: Subject File, Ronald Reagan Library; mention of High Frontier's own documentary mentioned in "Draft: Public Affairs Plan."

43. Bill Moyers, "Commentary (*The Day After* Controversy)," *CBS Evening News,* November 18, 1983; Peter Jennings and Falwell quotes from *World News Tonight,* November 18, 1983; Weber quoted in Wittner, *Toward Nuclear Abolition,* 187.

44. Report by Morton Dean, *CBS Evening News,* November 20, 1983.

45. Ibid.

46. "Notes from Meeting on 'The Day After,'" bullet point 5.

47. On ABC's first choices for White House representatives, see Sims to McFarlane and Gergen memo; in "Public Affairs Strategy for 'The Day After,'" Bush's name is scratched out and Schultz's is handwritten in.

48. ABC News, *Viewpoint,* November 20, 1983, accessed at Vanderbilt Television News Archive, transcribed by the author; portions of the program are now available on YouTube.

49. Quote cited in Perrine, *Film and the Nuclear Age,* 154, 175, as from "the cover of the videocassette version of the film distributed by ABC Video / Embassy Home Entertainment."

50. Reported by Dan Rather for *CBS Evening News,* Tom Brokaw for *NBC Nightly News,* and unnamed reporter for *ABC World News Tonight,* November 21, 1983, accessed at Vanderbilt Television News Archive, transcribed by the author.

51. Gergen to the President memo.

52. Quote on poll from Patrick Mannix, *The Rhetoric of Antinuclear Fiction: Persuasive Strategies in Novels and Films* (Lewisburg, PA: Bucknell University Press, 1992), 175, who cites data found in Robert D. McFadden, "Atomic War Film Spurs Nationwide Discussion," *New York Times,* November 22, 1983.

53. "Nationwide Survey by G. W. Professor Finds No Fallout from *The Day After,*" George Washington University press release, November 21, 1983, attached to "The Day After," memo, Dick Wirthlin to Bruce Chapman, November 21, 1983, folder "The Day After," box OA 11691, Bruce Chapman Files, Ronald Reagan Library.

54. On polling data, see Joseph Fromm, "The Day after *The Day After,*" *U.S. News and World Report* 5 (December 1983): 29; also cited in Mannix, *The Rhetoric of Antinuclear Fiction,* 81.

55. On Reagan's elusive private character, see Edmund Morris, *Dutch: A Memoir of Ronald Reagan;* on Reagan's supposed hatred of nuclear weapons, see Paul Lettow, *Ronald Reagan and His Quest to Abolish Nuclear Weapons* (New York: Random House, 2005).

Chapter 4. Weapons in Space

1. For the ratings, see www.gallup.com/poll/116677/presidential-approval-ratings-gallup-historical-statistics-trends.aspx.

2. Statistical Abstract of the United States, data from 1984 report via US Bureau of Labor Statistics, available online at www.census.gov/library/publications/1983/compendia/statab/104ed.html.

3. Daniel Wirls, *Buildup: The Politics of Defense in the Reagan Era* (Ithaca, NY: Cornell University Press, 1992), 148; "Address to the Nation on National Security, March 23, 1983," available online at http://www.reagan.utexas.edu/archives/speeches/1983/32383d.htm.

4. For examples from the "Reagan Victory School," see Peter Schweitzer, *Reagan's War: The Epic Story of His Forty-Year Struggle and Final Triumph over Communism* (New York: Random House, 2002); Paul Lettow *Ronald Reagan and His Quest to Abolish Nuclear Weapons* (New York: Random House, 2005); for more critical assessments of SDI, see Frances FitzGerald, *Way Out There in the Blue: Reagan, Star Wars, and the End of the Cold War* (New York: Simon and Schuster, 2000); Richard Rhodes, *Arsenals of Folly: The Making of the Nuclear Arms Race* (New York: Knopf, 2007).

5. Edward Linenthal, *Symbolic Defense: The Cultural Significance of the Strategic Defense Initiative* (Urbana: University of Illinois Press, 1989), xiii; Union of Concerned Scientists, newsletter, September 1986, included in memo, Charles Z. Wick to John Poindexter, October 24, 1986, ID#469629, ND018, WHORM: Subject File, Ronald Reagan Library.

6. Richard Stengel, "The Great Star Wars P.R. War: Kindergarten Imagery Obscures a Vital and Complex Debate," *Time,* December 9, 1985, 31–32.

7. Ronald Reagan, "Address to the Nation on Defense and National Security" March 23, 1983, available online at www.reagan.utexas.edu/archives/speeches/1983/32383d.htm.

8. Douglass Brinkley, ed., *The Reagan Diaries* (New York: Harper Perennial, 2007), 139–40.

9. On administration officials' surprise on learning of the SDI announcement, see Lou Cannon, *President Reagan: The Role of a Lifetime* (New York: Public Affairs, 2000),

286–87; FitzGerald, *Way Out There in the Blue*, 198–200; Leslie H. Gelb, "Aides Urged Reagan to Postpone Antimissile Ideas for More Study," *New York Times*, March 25, 1983, a source also cited in Richard Reeves, *Ronald Reagan: The Triumph of Imagination* (New York: Simon & Schuster, 2005), 147; see also Lou Cannon and David Hoffman, "President Overruled Advisors on Announcing Defense Plans," *Washington Post*, March 26, 1983.

10. On Reagan's tendency to conflate film storyline with reality, see Michael Paul Rogin, *Ronald Reagan, The Movie: And Other Episodes in Political Demonology* (Berkeley: University of California Press, 1987); on *Murder in the Air*, and quotations from it, see FitzGerald, *Way Out There in the Blue*, 22–25; Linenthal, *Symbolic Defense*, 6–7.

11. On the roots of the ABM treaty, see John Lewis Gaddis, *Strategies of Containment: A Critical Appraisal of American National Security Policy during the Cold War* (Oxford, UK: Oxford University Press, 2005), 322–26; on SDI as a response to the ABM treaty, see Cannon, *President Reagan*, 278–79.

12. FitzGerald, *Way Out There in the Blue*, 19–21. For a longer narrative on Reagan and the roots of SDI, see Lettow, *Ronald Reagan and His Quest to Abolish Nuclear Weapons*, 18–25; see also chapter section "Reagan and Missile Defense in the 1980 Campaign," 37–41.

13. On the Sentinel program, Safeguard, and ABM history, see Lawrence Freeman, *The Evolution of Nuclear Strategy* (New York: Palgrave Macmillan, 2003), 319–26; see also Wirls, *Buildup*, 138–40.

14. FitzGerald, *Way Out There in the Blue*, 121–23; Paul Boyer, "Selling Star Wars: Ronald Reagan's Strategic Defense Initiative," in *Selling War in a Media Age: The Presidency and Public Opinion in the American Century*, ed. Kenneth Osgood and Andrew Frank (Gainesville: University Press of Florida, 2010), 202–4.

15. On the roots of Brilliant Pebbles—the brainchild of Lowell Wood, who worked alongside Teller—see FitzGerald, *Way Out There in the Blue*, 135, 481–84.

16. Sanford Lakoff and Herbert F. York, *A Shield in Space? Technology, Politics, and the Strategic Defense Initiative* (Berkeley: University of California Press, 1989), 9–10; Wirls, *Buildup*, 145; on Graham's biographical information, see FitzGerald, *Way Out There in the Blue*, 125–27.

17. FitzGerald, *Way Out There in the Blue*, 132–33; Lakoff and York, *A Shield in Space?*, 10–11; Wirls, *Buildup*, 146.

18. On administration officials' pessimism, see FitzGerald, *Way Out There in the Blue*, 198–99; on Weinberger's appraisal, see Boyer, "Selling Star Wars," 5–7; Keyworth's remarks cited in Wirls, *Buildup*, 144.

19. On Graham's ignoring facts, see FitzGerald, *Way Out There in the Blue*, 125–27; on Graham's interest in ESP, see "An E.S.P. Gap," *Time*, January 23, 1984.

20. FitzGerald, *Way Out There in the Blue*, 132–37; Department of Defense quote from Herbert Reynolds, Office of the Under Secretary of Defense, "Point Paper on Global Ballistic Missile Defense," September 28, 1981, cited ibid., 142.

21. Linenthal, *Symbolic Defense*, 111–12.

22. Rogin, *Ronald Reagan, The Movie*, 42–43.

23. Daniel O. Graham and Gregory A. Fossedal, *A Defense That Defends: Blocking Nuclear Attack* (Old Greenwich, CT: Devin-Adair, 1983); Daniel O. Graham, *High Frontier: A Strategy for National Survival* (New York: Tom Doherty Associates, 1983), 42–43 (dedication, 6).

24. Letter, Daniel O. Graham to Karna Small, November 4, 1983, with attachment "High Frontier: Two Day Media Blitz, November 20, 21, 1983—Response to *The Day After*,"

ID# 183666, PR016–01, WHORM: Subject File, Ronald Reagan Library. Memo, David B. Waller to Fred F. Fielding, November 8, 1983, is included as an attachment in memo, David B. Waller to Fred Fielding, November 14, 1983, ID#183666CU, PR016–01, WHORM: Subject File, Ronald Reagan Library.

25. Letter, Ronald Reagan to Daniel O. Graham, June 3, 1983, case file 202239CU, PR 014–09, WHORM: Subject File, Ronald Reagan Library.

26. Letter, Fred F. Fielding to Daniel Graham, February 22, 1984, case file 202239CU, PR 014–09, WHORM: Subject File, Ronald Reagan Library.

27. "Star Spangled Sweepstakes" mailer, included in letter, Evelyn Mohr [private citizen] to President Ronald Reagan, August ID# 337322CU, PR014–09, WHORM: Subject File, Ronald Reagan Library.

28. On administration's stance on the sweepstakes, see memo, Hugh Hewitt to Fred F. Fielding, August 21, 1985, ID#337322CU, PR014–09, WHORM: Subject File, Ronald Reagan Library.

29. Daniel O. Graham, *A Defense That Defends* (1984), video, 27 min.; copy provided to the author by Edward Linenthal.

30. Although specific author attribution is missing, the UCS mission statement can be found in John Tirman, ed., *The Fallacy of Star Wars* (New York: Vintage Books, 1985), 294; on the UCS and the influence of the "New Left," see Kelly Moore, *Disrupting Science: Social Movements, American Scientists, and the Politics of the Military, 1945–1975* (Princeton, NJ: Princeton University Press, 2008), esp. chap. 6, "Doing 'Science for the People': Enactments of a New Left Politics of Science," 158–89.

31. Richard L. Garwin and Carl Sagan, "Ban Space Weapons," a petition reprinted in *Bulletin of the Atomic Scientists* 39.9 (November 1983): 2–3.

32. On Sagan's brush with death and response to SDI, see Keay Davidson, *Carl Sagan: A Life* (New York: John Wiley & Sons, 1999), 356–59—Sagan quote on 359; see also David Poundstone, *Carl Sagan: A Life in the Cosmos* (New York: Henry Holt, 1999), 300–301.

33. "17 Experts Urge a Ban on Outer-Space Arms," *New York Times,* March 27, 1983; see also a follow-up op-ed, Richard L. Garwin and Carl Sagan, "Space Weapons: Andropov and the American Petitioners," *New York Times,* May 18, 1983.

34. Letter, Henry W. Kendall to Ronald Reagan, May 20, 1983, ID#140203; letter, Christopher C. Kraft, Jr., to Craig Fuller, July 7, 1983, ID#154721; letter, John H. Hawes to Dr. Henry Kendall, August 16, 1985, ID# 293106; Union of Concerned Scientists to Ronald Reagan and General Secretary Michael [*sic*] Gorbachev, May 29, 1985, ID#304980, all ND018, WHORM: Subject File, Ronald Reagan Library.

35. Union of Concerned Scientists in cooperation with Massachusetts Teachers Association and National Education Association, *Choices: A Unit on Conflict and Nuclear War* (Washington, DC: National Education Association, 1983), included in letter, Henry W. Kendall to Ronald Reagan, July 6, 1983, ID#153688, ED003, WHORM: Subject File, Ronald Reagan Library; Reagan quoted in David Shribman, "Reagan Implies that the N.E.A. Lessons Are Aimed at Brainwashing Students," *New York Times,* July 6, 1983.

36. Kendall to Reagan, July 6, 1983.

37. Kendall quoted in United Press International, "700 Scientists Call for End to Research on 'Star Wars,'" *Los Angeles Times,* May 30, 1985.

38. Dean's request to meet with McFarlane is recorded in memo, [NCS Director of Arms Control] Sven Kraemer to Robert C. McFarlane, February 8, 1985, ID#298088, FG006–12, WHORM: Subject File, Ronald Reagan Library.

39. Ibid; letter, Ronald Reagan to Professor Eugene P. Wigner, June 27, 1985, ID# 325664, PR005–02, WHORM: Subject File, Ronald Reagan Library.

40. Memo, Sven Kraemer to Robert McFarlane, February 27, 1985, ID#298088, FG006–12, WHORM: Subject File, Ronald Reagan Library.

41. *Weapons in Space,* produced by Carl Sagan and Jon Lomberg, 1984, DVD provided to the author by Bob Derkach.

42. Edward Linenthal provided copies of both commercials to the author. In *Symbolic Defense,* Linenthal states that the "Crayola Ad" was sponsored by the "Coalition for the Strategic Defense Initiative," yet other reports cite the commercial originating from High Frontier, and Linenthal acknowledges High Frontier for providing the ad (108–9, 134 n. 25).

43. See Stengel, "The Great Star Wars P.R. War," 31–32.

44. Linenthal, *Symbolic Defense,* 111–12.

45. UCS commercials provided to the author by Edward Linenthal, May 20, 2011.

46. Robert Bissell, *NBC Nightly News,* May 30, 1985; *CBS Evening News,* November 14, 1985, quote found in Linenthal, *Symbolic Defense,* 112.

47. Graham misspoke: In the "Twinkle, Twinkle" ad, the child is a boy, not a girl; see also Linenthal, *Symbolic Defense,* 112.

48. *Spies Like Us,* produced by Brian Glazer, directed by John Landis, 102 min. (Aar Films and Warner Bros. Pictures, 1985); *Real Genius,* produced by Brian Glazer, directed by Martha Coolidge, 108 min. (Delphi III Productions, 1985).

49. Stengel, "The Great Star Wars P.R War."

50. Bernard Gwertzman, "'Star Wars' Is Not a Bargaining Chip, U.S. Says," *New York Times,* December 24, 1984; Hedrick Smith, "'Star Wars' Battle: Moscow and Congress Increase the Pressure on Reagan," *New York Times,* September 26, 1985; Abrahamson had briefly considered hiring Daniel Graham as an upper-level SDIO staffer, but he assessed High Frontier staffer Lowell L. Wood's proposals for "smart rocks" (later dubbed "brilliant pebbles"), X-ray, and chemical laser weapons as more futuristic than realistic.

51. Abrahamson quoted in FitzGerald, *Way Out There in the Blue,* 248; FitzGerald cites this quote as in the valuable collection Philip M. Boffey, William J. Broad, Leslie H. Gelb, Charles Mohr, and Holcomb B. Noble, *Claiming the Heavens: The New York Times Complete Guide to the Star Wars Debate* (New York: Times Books, 1988), 64–65.

52. Note, "Tom G." [Thomas F. Gibson III, Office of Public Affairs] to Office of Communications Assistant Pat Buchanan, October 28, 1986, ID#440212, ND018, WHORM: Subject File, Ronald Reagan Library.

53. Proxmire quote from *Face the Nation,* December 14, 1984, transcript, p. 14, folder "Nuclear Winter," Box 90570, Ronald Lehman Files, Ronald Reagan Library.

54. Author unattributed (although handwriting notes that Richard Perle, as well as Abrahamson, would have seen a copy), "Course for SDI," ID#448445, ND018, WHORM: Subject File, Ronald Reagan Library; "Concept Paper Draft: U.S. Forces and Allied Defense Initiative," ID#459997, ND018, WHORM: Subject File, Ronald Reagan Library.

55. "Tom G." to Buchanan.

56. Author unattributed, "Course for SDI," ID#448445, ND018, WHORM: Subject File, Ronald Reagan Library.

57. On SDI coverage in network news, see Robert Karl Manoff, "Modes of War and Modes of Social Address: The Text of SDI," *Journal of Communication* 39.1 (Winter 1989): 60. The railgun prototype story is featured in Malcolm W. Browne, "The Star Wars Spinoff,"

New York Times, August 24, 1986; see also part 3 of the PBS series *War and Peace in the Nuclear Age,* "Reagan's Shield," aired April 10, 1989, available on YouTube.

58. John Tirman, ed., *Empty Promise: The Growing Case against Star Wars* (Boston: Beacon Press, 1986), x; Union of Concerned Scientists, *The False Frontier* (1986), videocassette, accessed via Wisconsin Department of Public Instruction, Madison.

59. The ADPA went through numerous transformations. It was founded in Washington after World War I as the Army Ordnance Association, but in 1948 it became the American Ordnance Association; in 1965 it merged with the Armed Forces Chemical Association. The organization officially changed its name to the American Defense Preparedness Association in 1973. In 1997 the ADPA merged with the National Security Industrial Association to become the National Defense Industrial Association. See "History of NDIA" online at www.ndia.org/ABOUTUS/Pages/HistoryofNDIA.aspx.

60. Memo, [NSC Executive Secretary] Grant S. Green to James F. Lemon, "Secretary of Defense's Draft Remarks at the American Defense Preparedness Association, May 20, 1987," ID 504620, FG013, WHORM: Subject File, Ronald Reagan Library.

61. Memo, Steve Steiner / Bob Linhard to Frank C. Carlucci, "ADPA Questions and Proposed Responses, May 12, 1987," May 11, 1987, ID# 504032, FG006–12, WHORM: Subject File, Ronald Reagan Library. Filming took place on May 17.

62. Ibid.

63. Ibid.

64. On funding amounts and production of *SDI: A Prospect for Peace,* see "Washington Talk: Briefing; 'Star Wars,' a Sequel?," *New York Times,* October 20, 1987; the story reports that "later a local television station has agreed to show the film," presumably once. Memo, Grant S. Green to Anthony R. Dolan, October 16, 1987, ID# 540829, PR011, RRL.

65. Estimates on SDI funding before the ADPA's involvement are $1.2 billion in 1984 and $2.5 billion in 1985. See Wirls, *Buildup,* 155; by century's end, BMD federal spending may have topped $50 billion; see Collins, *Transforming America,* 203; see also John E. Pike, Bruce G. Blair, and Stephen I. Schwartz, "Defending against the Bomb," in *Atomic Audit: The Costs and Consequences of U.S. Nuclear Weapons since 1940,* ed. Stephen I. Schwartz (Washington, DC: Brookings Institution Press, 1998), 291.

66. Linenthal, *Symbolic Defense,* xiii, 89.

67. Ibid., xiii.

Conclusion

1. On Reagan's cowboy analogy, see Frances FitzGerald, *Way Out There in the Blue: Reagan, Star Wars, and the End of the Cold War* (New York: Simon and Schuster, 2000), 28.

2. James Graham Wilson, *The Triumph of Improvisation* (Ithaca, NY: Cornell University Press, 2012), 23–24, 63.

3. Christopher Andrews, *For the President's Eyes Only: Secret Intelligence and the American Presidency from Washington to Bush* (New York: Harper Perennial, 1995), 476; Reagan quote from a November 18 diary entry; see Douglas Brinkley, ed., *The Reagan Diaries* (New York: HarperCollins, 2007), 199.

4. Reagan's "rebellion" against his anticommunist cabinet members is the focus of James Mann's *The Rebellion of Ronald Reagan: A History of the End of the Cold War* (New York: Viking Press, 2009).

5. On the importance of Reagan's working relationship with Gorbachev, see Melvyn P. Leffler, *For the Soul of Mankind: The United States, The Soviet Union, and the Cold War* (New York: Hill and Wang, 2007), 338–450.

6. Brinkley, *The Reagan Diaries,* 185–86; on people in the Pentagon being "crazy," see Ronald Reagan, *An American Life* (New York: Pocket Books, 1990), 586; on this diary entry being Reagan's only clear example of being greatly depressed (in the wake of *The Day After*), see Edmund Morris, *Dutch: A Memoir of Ronald Reagan* (New York: Random House, 1999), 498.

7. Lou Cannon, *President Reagan: The Role of a Lifetime* (New York: Public Affairs, 2000), 217.

8. Fred Kaplan, *Dark Territory: The Secret History of Cyber War* (New York: Simon & Schuster, 2016), 1–4.

9. Tower quoted in Andrew Rosenthal, "Tower Declares 'Star Wars' Shield Can't Be Complete," *New York Times,* January 27, 1989; on the context of this quote, Brilliant Pebbles, and Carlucci's defense cuts for SDI, see Rebecca Slayton, *Arguments That Count: Physics, Computing, and Missile Defense, 1949–2012* (Cambridge, MA: MIT Press, 2013), 196–97.

10. Slayton, *Arguments That Count,* 199–226; Paul Harris, "Bush Plans New Nuclear Weapons: 'Bunker-Buster' Bombs Set to End 10-Year Research Ban," *Observer,* November 29, 2003.

11. O. Brian Toon, interview by the author, January 25, 2011; Ann Druyan, interview by the author, February 8, 2010; Naomi Oreskes and Erik M. Conway, *Merchants of Doubt: How a Handful of Scientists Obscured the Truth on Issues from Tobacco Smoke to Global Warming* (New York: Bloomsbury Press, 2010), 65; S. Fred Singer and Dennis T. Avery, *Unstoppable Global Warming* (New York: Rowman & Littlefield, 2007).

12. Alan Robock and Owen Brian Toon, "Local Nuclear War, Global Suffering," *Scientific American* 302 (2009): 74–81; Barack Obama, "Opinion: How We Can Make Our Vision of a World without Nuclear Weapons a Reality," *Washington Post,* March 30, 2016.

13. Richard Rhodes, *The Twilight of the Bombs: Recent Challenges, New Dangers, and the Prospects for a World without Nuclear Weapons* (New York: Knopf, 2010), 283–303.

14. See *Bulletin of Atomic Scientists,* especially "Nuclear Notebook: Nuclear Arsenals of the World," although updates on the status of global arsenals are periodic: http://thebulletin.org/nuclear-notebook-multimedia; quote about Putin: Hans M. Kristensen, "Russian Nuclear Forces, 2016," *Bulletin of Atomic Scientists,* May 3, 2016, http://thebulletin.org/2016/may/russian-nuclear-forces-20169394.

Index